S-1
A True Short Story

OF A
CLOSED NEUROPSYCHIATRIC
MENTAL WARD DURING
THE FORGOTTEN WAR – KOREA.

A. PATRICK SHAW

TATE PUBLISHING
AND ENTERPRISES, LLC

Published by Tate Publishing & Enterprises, LLC
127 E. Trade Center Terrace | Mustang, Oklahoma 73064 USA
1.888.361.9473 | www.tatepublishing.com

Tate Publishing is committed to excellence in the publishing industry. The company reflects the philosophy established by the founders, based on Psalm 68:11,
"The Lord gave the word and great was the company of those who published it."

Book design copyright © 2014 by Tate Publishing, LLC. All rights reserved.
Cover design by Nikolai Purpura
Interior design by Joana Quilantang

Published in the United States of America

ISBN: 978-1-63268-212-3
1. Psychology / Psychopathology / Post-Traumatic Stress Disorder (PTSD)
2. Psychology / History
14.07.21

ACKNOWLEDGMENTS

First, I would like to thank my dear wife of nearly fifteen years, Stephanie. Without her help and support I could not have written this amazing true story. She corrected my grammar and advised me with her valued opinion of all my thoughts as I transposed them to create this book. God has blessed me so much with Stephanie in my life. We have had many joys and very few sad times in our marriage. This book was not possible without her input.

Going on the Internet helped reading and then remembering the events that took place during the Korean War. Some of the publications were:

The California State Military Museum
(Letterman Army Hospital)
Wikipedia (Letterman Army Hospital history)
National Park Services (Presidio of San Francisco)
www.infoplease.com (American War Casualties)
Korean War Educator, "Topic: Health Issues"
Psychiatry in the Korean War, Dr. A.
Glass and Dr. Frank James

CONTENTS

PROLOGUE

This is a nonfiction account of two important years in my life during the time I was drafted into the army during the Korean War. First, my time in a "crash" six-week basic training program reduced from fourteen weeks because the war was going so badly and soldiers were needed practically overnight in Korea. Soon after this began my time at Letterman Army Hospital in S-1, a closed neuropsychiatric mental ward that was a "virtual snake pit." My time at S-1 changed my life.

All the names have been changed because many of the people are probably still living. Many, I am sure, have lived very successful lives and others not too successful since their time at S-1.

INTRODUCTION OF S-1

S-1 is the true short story of a closed neuropsychiatric mental ward in Letterman Army Hospital at the Presidio of San Francisco "during the forgotten war—Korea."

A BIT OF HISTORY ABOUT S-1

In the beginning the persecution and martyrdom or dominance by the army personnel who actually ran the day-to-day operation at S-1 created a dangerous environment for the patients. When I arrived at S-1, it was a horrible snake-pit asylum but by the time I left it had become a superb psychiatric rehabilitation center for mentally ill patients.

I did not realize at the time but I now know that it was predestined that I come to S-1. I had no idea that I had a purpose to be an active contributor, along with others, to bring compassion and understanding to the patients. Compassion requires action and in time I did take action. In the beginning I was just another fresh, very young twenty-two-year-old, but boy, did I mature quickly! Back in the '50s mental patients were thought to be a forlorn and frightening group of people. They were not to be associated with or really helped in anyway. The idea was to "put them in a room, lock the door, and throw away the key." No one wanted to be near them, see them, or even touch them. It was as if they had a contagious disease-like leprosy. The mentally ill were literally like lepers from the Bible—banished from society.

I purposely and for good reasons have not used real names of the soldiers, patients, doctors, nurses, or medics that I met and worked with during my time in service. The events that took place are all from my memory of years ago. The exact dates may vary slightly but are very close to the time of the incidents and events that took place.

The life-changing, fascinating story of S-1 will come a little later. I feel it is important that you know some things about my history and background leading up to S-1. Then all the things that went on at S-1 that I was personally involved in will be much more important. I am not a doctor nor have I ever had any formal training about neuropsychiatric patients, but my many months at S-1 were very defining in my journey in life. As Ralph Waldo Emerson said, "Life is a journey not a destination!" This is a story of a meaningful part of my journey.

Why a Story about S-1?

My wife, Stephanie, and I recently were in San Francisco on business. (At that time Stephanie and I had only been married for twelve years as we both had been widowed previously.) We had some free time before our appointments began and I wanted to show her a bit of the area where I had lived and worked many years ago during the Korean War. While in the army as a medic, I was stationed at the Letterman Army Hospital at the Presidio. I was shocked at how much the area had changed. If you have never been to this part of San Francisco, it is one of the wealthiest and most beautiful areas in San Francisco. I was absolutely amazed to see how everything had changed. There is no hospital or colonial homes that army colonels lived in. Everything that I remembered from the past is gone. It was beautiful when I was there but it is even more beautiful now. But all had changed—the hospital, Letterman General Hospital, the S-1 building, the closed mental ward where I was stationed as a medical corpsman, and also the colonels' colonial mansions were all gone. The entire complex of the army headquarters and supporting buildings had disappeared. We then drove down to the area by the bay area. There were no barracks, theater, PX, mess hall cafeteria, or the mental patient open ward. All were gone, and I am sure many people today have forgotten or new people visiting the Presidio have any knowledge that they ever existed. I told Stephanie that I must write a book about Letterman and most importantly about my life at S-1. People should not forget the Korean War, and particularly I do not want to forget the evolution of mental health and the treatment of patients in S-1 (the closed psychiatric mental ward). All of this happened during the early1950s. I had experiences there that few people ever have had in a lifetime. The experiences were brutal, the experiences were heartbreaking, and the experiences were life-changing. But when I left S-1, it was a loving, wonderful experience that I will never forget. Here are my thoughts and many, many memories.

THE KOREAN WAR

To begin with, the Korean War was about North Korea trying to occupy South Korea and make Korea into one country. North Korea was a communist country and the North Koreans were war mongers. But South Korea was trying to become a democracy. In the winter of 1951 the Korean War was not going at all well for the South Koreans and the USA. The period of December 1950 and early January 1951 found the morale of the United Nations' troops, and in particular the United States troops, at the lowest possible ebb. In fact, previously it had been called a "police action" in early 1950 by President Truman. The US troops were supposedly there as only advisors to assist in training the South Korean army. Most of the US troops were World War II veterans with tremendous experience in fighting the enemy. But our troops were totally ill-equipped with complete lack of weapons, ammunition, clothing, and even enough rations to fight the enemy. By late November 1950, the early expectations of the South Korean's early victory was completely gone. In December 1950, South Korea with our advisory assistance had been bitterly defeated. In

October 1950, the Chinese leader, Mao Zedong, ordered hundreds of thousands of his troops to Korea to aid the North Koreans. These troops from China were well trained with great equipment, fire power, and the proper clothing for the anticipated severe winter as it was one of the most severe winters in Korean history. It was a total disaster for our troops. We had 150,000 American troops at this time in Korea and we were 88 percent of the total troops from twenty nations. But the brutal conditions in Korea were never known by the American people. Most of this information never came back to the USA because this happened before TV publicized such events. It was not until the Vietnam War that TV told America what was going on in the rest of the world, day by day, minute by minute. The United States' high command was totally distraught over the losses of the previously hard-won territories. The cold weather was unbelievable. It produced a defeatist attitude in the troops and there were many rumors that Korea would be evacuated. The conditions in Korea could not have been worse. Because we were ill-equipped, this war was a disaster. It had become "decision time" as to whether we should continue in this war or pull out. The decision was made in Washington DC to quickly increase training of manpower to be sent to Korea, along with food, clothing, equipment, and munitions.

MY BACKGROUND

In January 1951 I was drafted at the most critical period of the Korean War. But first let me give you a little bit of my history about myself before I was drafted. I was living at home in Minneapolis with my mother. My parents were in the process of a divorce. I was working as a sales trainee for Lasher Carpet Company, a very large wholesale floor covering company. I had left the University of Minnesota less than a year before. I had started in pre-veterinary medicine at the university six months before I graduated from John Marshall High School. My grades were excellent, my high school load was light, so I was allowed to start early at the university. Marshall was one block outside the campus at the university and I lived a mile away on River Road. I was very fortunate to be in the first veterinary medicine class at the University of Minnesota. After extensive testing to be in veterinary school, I ended up being the only "city boy" who was in this first class. The other twenty-nine were all "country boys" from the vast farmlands of Minnesota. The grades in each class were on a curve. For example, I remember that in my poultry husbandry class an A was 99 or 100, a

B was 97 or 98, a C was 95 or 96, below a 95 was failure. With all the farm boys in the class, I had a 94. It was really tough! Naturally, I had to take the class over. I was fortunate and received a 97 the next time.

It was even tougher at home. My parents were in the middle of a bad divorce after thirty-three years of marriage. I was the youngest of four children and I had three older sisters but none at home. Studying was impossible at home for various reasons I would rather not discuss. I also worked at a gas station part time after school every day for three to five hours. My childhood sweetheart, Bev Taylor, lived way on the other side of Minneapolis (fifteen miles away). Bev and I had met at a college day conference. This conference was for any students from high schools in Minneapolis area planning on going to the U of M. I went with friends from my high school, Marshall, and Bev with friends from her school, Southwest High. At the general assembly I saw this gorgeous girl with her girlfriends and I had all of us from my school sit in front of them. Everyone had a nametag so I knew her name was Beverly Taylor. I asked her lots of questions but she was totally not interested in me. I had played tennis against the state champ from her high school. He beat me 6-1, 6-1. I will not go into more details but she finally went out with me and we had a few years of courtship. Then after we graduated from our respective high schools, we became engaged.

I had no car at that time so I had to take a streetcar to work and also to see Bev only on weekends. I could have had a partial scholarship in tennis and/or wrestling at the university, but they did not allow much financial assistance in minor sports at that time.

So because of the situation at home I finally dropped out of school and applied and secured the job as a sales trainee at the flooring company. My master plan was to go back to school sometime in the future. But now that I was working full time, I was able to buy a car—a 1949 yellow with red interior Ford convertible. I bought the car from my sister Zoe and her husband Al. Al had been promoted to sales manager of his company and along with the promotion Al got a company car. Zoe and Al had small children and they thought the convertible in Minnesota was not too practical with kids, but I loved it! I was also able to see Bev more often now that I had transportation. (We did get married while I was in service; more about that later.)

That's enough for now about my personal life before being drafted and eventually about the main story of this book—S-1.

DRAFTED IN ARMY,
FORT RILEY, KANSAS

I was drafted in January 1951 at the height of the disaster in Korea. I was sent by train to Fort Riley, Kansas, the "hellhole" of the army training bases in the USA! At the time I was very excited about fighting for my country but sad to leave Bev, my family, and my new job. Fort Riley was a training facility during WWI and WWII, and it looked like it because it was really an ugly place. Not at all like I had seen in movies about army training with all the rah-rah! The first two weeks at Fort Riley were indoctrination and testing for various capabilities. I guess this is the same routine and procedures they have been doing for fifty years with new recruits. We had physicals and our heads were shaved. Then we were issued army uniforms such as underwear, fatigues, boots, wool coats, hats, insignias, and dress Ike jacket uniforms, plus towels, blankets, sheets, and a pillow of course. We received all the necessary stuff to make us into soldiers quickly. And we were civilians no longer. There were probably 1,000 of us new draftees from all over the midwest and south to Missouri, Kansas, Texas, and Oklahoma. Because the war was going so badly, anyone twenty to twenty-six years old who could breathe was drafted. You may think I am kidding but we had young men with wooden legs, many missing an arm, some with one eye, and others missing a hand or some fingers. This was pretty common. During this two-week "weed-out" period, those with wooden legs, missing an eye, and/or missing arms were returned home. But the rest were put into six-week accelerated training classes and then being shipped quickly to Korea because the war was going so badly. Previously the regular army training was a fourteen-week training program and then assignment somewhere. We were told from the first day that training would be twenty-four hours a day. Sleep would be no more than four to six hours any night. We would have night fighting with intense training in winter conditions because it would be these conditions when we arrived in Korea. Live ammo would be fired over us on the infiltration courses. We were told from the beginning that we would be treated like animals and that we would become robots. So when we were told to respond to an order, we charged forward without thinking. When we heard an order or command, we were to follow the order without thinking. When some officer or non-com officer said jump, we were to answer "How high?" Lastly, we were told that we were all nothing but numbers and not human beings. They wanted us to be like wild animals in a circus. If we did not react properly, we would be whipped and beaten. Well, the next six weeks was everything they said and more. "It was hell on earth."

I was assigned to company C as in Charlie. Because my last name was Shaw, I was assigned to the fourth barracks, the D barracks in the company C. I had an upper bunk on the second floor of the barracks. My bunkmate was John from Baton Rouge, Louisiana. John was a real Cajun in speech and actions. He was about five-foot-seven, weighed about 175 pounds, and was all muscle. We became friends from the minute we met. We were told in the barracks that the first thing that we had to do was make our beds properly as we were shown in indoctrination class. We had to make the bed so tight that a quarter would flip on the bed. Edges of the tucked-in sheet and blanket were to be perfectly mitered, the pillow smooth without wrinkles. Each of our lockers had to be perfectly arranged for inspection. We had a filthy-mouthed corporal in charge of the platoon barking out orders. He told everyone that he had enlisted in 1944, he had fought in every battle in the world, and he personally had won every battle. He was so full of himself and every other word was "motherf——," "cocks——," or all I want to see are "assholes and elbows." If we did anything wrong or spoke out of place, it was KP duty to peel potatoes or latrine duty to clean toilets and wash the floor on our knees with a scrub brush. I remember at least twice during the six-week training course this "animal" actually pushed two different trainees down the stairs to the first floor for something they did wrong. One actually broke his wrist. I made up my mind that if he ever touched me he would regret it, but it never happened. His name was Corporal Bertrum, nicknamed "The Animal." He hated draftees and said so. He said that only career-enlisted men made really good soldiers. All of us wanted to prove to this "jackass" that he was wrong about draftees.

The first night in the barracks it snowed about six inches. In the morning the top bunks, like mine, were covered with at least an inch of snow. The roof probably was the original from WWI, certainly not replaced since WWII. We were up and dressed by 5:30 a.m. with reveille (bugle call) at 5:15 a.m. We had fifteen minutes to shave, shower, and the other "s," plus get dressed. We lined up outside our barracks in four rows with ten men each. In company C we had four platoons with forty men in each platoon making a total of 160 men in each company. If everyone in each platoon was not outside by 5:30 a.m. properly dressed and standing "at attention," they were assigned KP or latrine duty starting at once. Then each platoon marched to chow at the company mess hall. Platoon A went in first to breakfast, then platoon B was next and so forth. I was in fourth platoon, or D, so we were the last to eat. By the time we got in the chow line, they were out of half the food. Frankly, the food was so bad that it really did not make much difference. The following day, B platoon ate first, and so forth until we had cycled all of the four platoons and started over. After a week of this routine, friends of friends from other barracks would "buck the chow line." An example was our turn, fourth platoon or D barracks, was to be first to eat on a particular day, and friends from A or B platoon of certain men or kids in our barracks would squeeze in our line beside their friends from our barracks to eat first that day. This went on time after time with a group of Spanish, tough kids from Texas. Everyone called them "wetbacks" or "spics" (not nice but true). They were bullies and arrogant little guys and felt they could do anything, and they tried everything. Well, we put up with this for about two weeks, and with all the intense training and all the pressure we were getting a little "uptight." One day at dinner this occurred and there were at least ten of these little monsters "bucking the chow line" ahead of John and myself. John asked them to go back to their own platoons. John then said that this "bucking the chow line" was stopping now and never again to do this during the rest of our basic training. Well, they laughed at John and said something not too nice in Spanish. And then one of them pushed John really hard. Well, John hauled off and hit him and knocked him out. Then all ten of his friends piled on John so I handed my glasses to another draftee and pitched in the fight to help John. Five minutes later all ten were on the ground crying and some bleeding just a little. John and I were standing together literally untouched. About then the Master Sergeant over the entire company arrived. The ten babies, of course, said we started the fight because we did not like Spanish people and we did not like "spics." Guess what nationality the sergeant was? His name was Gonzales. John and I were immediately assigned to KP and latrine duty for two weeks. The nice little Mexicans received nothing. But from then on they never "bucked the chow line" of barracks 4 or D again.

Fourteen weeks' training packed into six weeks was all rough and tumble. Every weekend but the last two John and I were on KP or latrine duty. We also questioned some orders and decisions by the non-coms. This was also something you did not do either, or it's KP and latrine duty again. An example of this was that many times we double-timed with rifles over our heads. I asked once why we were doing this because it would not be done in combat. The non-com's answer was that, "You just do as you are told, soldier! Or you have KP duty again."

BAYONET PRACTICE

One time the entire company was out in the open parade ground area. We had about six feet of space completely around each of us to practice the bayonet movements. The captain in charge of the entire company was on a stage in front of everyone demonstrating how to use a bayonet in hand-to-hand combat. He yelled out, "Does everyone understand this maneuver?" Everyone yelled, "Yes, sir," except me. I was concentrating so hard on the maneuver and watching and listening so intently that I said, "uh-huh." Master Sergeant Gonzales was standing near me and screamed, "Soldier, you have disrespected the commanding officer. Soldier, you double time with your M1 rifle over your head until I tell you to stop." So I started to double time with my rifle and bayonet attached over my head. The rifle and bayonet together weighed about eleven to twelve pounds—it was something else. After about ten minutes, the bayonet practice stopped and everyone went to lunch except me still double timing with my rifle, bayonet, and the master sergeant nearby. About ten to fifteen minutes later I fell flat on my face from exhaustion. The sergeant came over and kicked me really hard in the side and said, "Get up, soldier, and double time, you worthless son of a bitch." I said to him, "Shoot me! I don't care. I can't double time any longer." I was totally exhausted. He kicked me one more time and walked away.

I never said uh-huh again but lots of yes, sirs. But he did not give me any more KP duty because my schedule was full of them already.

RIFLE RANGE

Fortunately, I had hunted with my father since I was eight years old; first squirrels and then deer as I got older. My dad was an avid hunter and gun collector and he taught me to be a pretty good marksman. So I excelled on the firing range. Some of the other draftees did not do so well and yet others became superb marksmen. Some had never seen or shot a rifle before being drafted but they became really good—even better than I was. On the bad side, one day the lieutenant was walking back and forth behind us when we were in a kneeling position and shooting at the targets fifty yards away. The lieutenant stopped and screamed at a soldier about how stupid he was and what a lousy shot. The soldier was so high-strung and uptight that he turned and fired his rifle at the officer and accidentally shot him. He then fired again and hit another soldier too. His gun was then grabbed away. He started screaming, "What have I done? What have I done?" Fortunately, neither the officer nor the other soldier died. The soldier who did the shooting was processed out of service soon after the incident. By the way, he had only three fingers on his shooting hand! We will never know if the missing fingers or his nerves caused the accidents.

Another time there was a similar incident, only this one was much worse. We were using .50 caliber stationary machine guns and a sergeant was screaming at another soldier. The soldier turned to look at the sergeant and then turned around and fired his machine gun, killing, I believe, the sergeant and three other soldiers. Why do I say "I believe"? Because this was all hush-hush. It was possible someone lived but I do not think so. They all looked dead to me. We were all high-strung from night fighting every night, lack of sleep, and being bombarded mentally by the non-coms and officers. Quite a few soldiers cracked up and were hospitalized. The soldier who did the shooting was supposedly being prosecuted but we never did hear the outcome. Again, everything was kept hush-hush.

INFILTRATION COURSE

Another group of disasters happened on the infiltration course. Live ammo was used on this course. We were all told this and told to keep our heads and asses down as we crawled on our stomachs with our M1s. We, of course, wore helmets, but a .50 caliber bullet would penetrate a helmet easily. I understood we lost a total of eight draftees who were killed on this course over the six-week period. It was all kept top secret so it is possible that a few may have survived. In each instance the wounded or dead were immediately removed from the course—but to where? None of this was ever discussed or to our knowledge was on the radio or published in the news. Many draftees had small radios that we listened to in our bunks but no one ever heard about any of the incidents ever happening.

By this time there was a total of twelve possibly killed in action during basic training—but not in Korea yet! Besides the twelve possibly killed between firing range and infiltration course, most all the draftees with one eye, missing a hand, etc., were weeded out. We lost a bunch with pneumonia and other sicknesses because of the cold weather, night-fighting maneuvers. Also nervous breakdowns were numerous. Many men sustained broken arms and a few had broken legs. We started training with 160 in our company and ended up with less than 100—ninety-seven to be exact. We were known as the jinxed company by the other companies, and it was true. Everyone shied away from us. None of this was ever published or on radio news programs. This was all part of the intense training and I guess was to be expected if the high command was going to rush troops to Korea with all possible speed.

NIGHT FIGHTING

Night fighting was sometimes lots of fun. We would battle another company. The battle would be won when one or other captured the opponent's headquarters. One company wore red pullovers or vests and the other yellow. We used fake ammo for these night fights. If you were captured or shot, you were through for the night. We actually used snowballs instead of hand grenades. If you were hit with a snowball and a second teammate verified the hit, you were out. (Our C company, even being shorthanded in personnel, were never defeated in one of these mock battles. So we must have done something right. Maybe the other companies were afraid of us, being jinxed and all.) The battles usually lasted two to three hours. It was all remindful of playing capture the flag when we were all kids.

KP (KITCHEN POLICE) DUTY

KP duty was quite an experience. As I said previously, John and I had KP every weekend except the last two during the six-week basic training cycle. John and I peeled what seemed to be millions of bushels of potatoes each weekend. Plus we opened hundreds of little cans of corn, beans, peaches, and green beans with the crudest opener. The opener had a sharp pointed blade, really strange-looking object. We were shown how to use it. We got blistered hands from all the cans we opened. I often wondered why we did not have five-gallon cans of all these different vegetables.

The only advantage to KP was that we got to eat first—even though the food was terrible. I lost weight not because of the rigorous training but the lack of good food. Grits were served with every meal. I had never eaten them before the army. I still, to this day, hate grits.

MAIL CALL [NOTE TO LAYOUT: SUBHEADING1]

All any of us looked forward to was mail call to see if our mothers had sent a care package of goodies. I was very fortunate because I got boxes from my mother, one of my sisters, and Bev. Bev's mother was "Betty Crocker." (True story—Bev's mother made all the cake recipes for Betty Crocker and she was the only tester in Minneapolis. Remember General Mills Headquarters is still in Minneapolis. I used to kid Bev that the only reason I fell in love with her was for her mother's cakes. My mother was a great cook but never made cakes; she always made pies three times a week plus cookies and homemade donuts. Every new cake mix that Betty Crocker introduced Agnes Taylor—Bev's mother—had to approve the cake recipe. She really had a famous reputation.)

MISSING HOME

I mentioned the care packages from everyone and how great they were. Some of the soldiers had no relatives sending packages so the rest of us shared our goodies with them. I probably received more than anyone else and it was fantastic. I cannot say how much I missed home. I know I shed a few tears at night in my bunk after lights were out. I felt like I would never see home again and would be in Korea very soon. The environment at Fort Riley was so terrible—far beyond anything I thought possible. I thought of home and my life before the army. Fortunately, in spite of my parents being in the middle of a divorce, my life at home was pretty darn good. Unfortunately, you do not appreciate all the great things in your life until they are gone. I was madly in love with Bev. She was a beautiful, brilliant young lady. I wrote her daily how much I loved her and was looking forward to our future together and how I knew God was watching over me. I read the Bible every day and it really helped. I said my prayers constantly for guidance. I tried to rationalize that this was just the army non-com's job. But why not treat us as humans? The meanness toward the recruits was something that I could not understand. I actually said a prayer for them occasionally. Bev's letters back to me were great. She told me about everything at home and how much she loved me.

LATRINE DUTY

John and I did latrine duty at night before going to bed. Everyone now showered at night because fifteen minutes is not enough time in the morning. We each had our own bucket of soap and a brush and old towels to wipe up afterward because mops were not allowed. I cleaned so many toilets that I got it down to science.

John and I soon learned in time to become invisible. When we lined up in formation, we always stayed in the back. We tried to never say or comment on anything—we became invisible. Remember, "Speak no evil, see no evil, and hear no evil." It finally worked! We got the last two weekends free to go into town, to church or whatever.

GUARD DUTY

Along with our other important duties we were assigned guard duty. We marched back and forth in front of our barracks with our M1 rifles on our shoulders for six hours straight. We were picked at random for this duty and a few other assignments. Usually those in the front row were always picked for these duties, so John and I stayed in the back as much as possible.

WEEKEND IN KANSAS

On my first weekend without KP duty, I went into the closest town, Manhattan, Kansas, on a Saturday afternoon, and I had a great meal at a restaurant. John was not feeling well so he stayed in the barracks. I had to go back to camp each night because I did not have money enough to stay at a hotel in town. The following day, Sunday, I went to a Methodist church for services. I was in uniform and after church I was invited to dinner at the home of one of the members. They told me that very few servicemen ever went to church on their days off training. The meal was great and the family was wonderful. They invited me back the following Sunday and I said I would try to come to church again and see them. Unfortunately, the next weekend some of the guys wanted to go to another little town close by where there was an amusement park. So John and I agreed to go with them.

MY PHYSICAL CONDITION

I will say that at the end of six weeks, I was solid muscle! I did hundreds of push-ups (which I despised). We ran double-time daily for up to two hours. At least once a week we packed everything in our duffel bags, strapped all sixty pounds of the bag on our backs, and ran for two miles—of course with our nine-pound M1 rifles.

TRAINING ENDS

I was promoted to private first class and earned $5.00 more a month—from $59.00 a month to $64.00. Then shortly after I became a PFC with one stripe, the promotions were frozen unless you were fighting in Korea. Well, I expected to be in Korea very soon. One last thing about the non-coms in basic training was that on payday, after we were paid in cash, the sergeant asked for money for the officer's club and the non-com clubhouse. He expected $5.00 from every soldier. If you did not pay, you received more KP, guard duty, and latrine duty. So we all gave $5.00—and that's a lot when you only make $59.00 per month. I have often wondered what he did with all that money.

Our company was assigned to a temporary interim facility and then to be assigned overseas orders. We were given shots for malaria and other diseases. Many got sick from the shots. I was fortunate and I did not have anything but a sore arm. My overseas' orders came through one day and I was to leave in two days by truck to then go to the nearest port to leave for Korea. But the following day my overseas orders were changed and I was to be sent to University of Northwestern to veterinary school. (The army still had a horse cavalry at that time and needed veterinarians.) The next day my orders were pulled again. Because of my small medical background, I was assigned to be sent to Brooke Army Hospital at Fort Sam Houston in San Antonio, Texas. I was to go to medical school to train to become an army medic. So I said good-bye to my friends in the fourth platoon, particularly John who was going on to Korea.

BROOKE ARMY HOSPITAL,
SAN ANTONIO, TEXAS

After being at Fort Riley, Fort Sam Houston and Brooke Army Hospital was a fantastic complex. The quarters for medical trainees were excellent. The food was superb and the treatment by superiors was done with respect. The area around the complex was very, very nice. All in all it was a great place.

MED I CLASSES

Classes were much like going back to high school. The class sizes were about thirty-five to forty, not like college where I had 500 in my chemistry class. First, we learned about the human body and all living organs. The classes were not difficult as I had studied most of the same subjects in high school along with biology, chemistry, and other related courses. Plus many of my classes at the University of Minnesota in pre-vet medicine were the same as the pre-med classes. So I excelled. My grades were the highest in the class.

We then studied the following:

- When to give shots
- How to give shots
- Taking blood samples
- How to give blood
- Preparation of a wound
- Fixing wounds of all types
- How to handle quickly the wounded
- How to handle soldiers in shock
- Handling patient who has broken an arm, leg, etc.
- Eyes, ears, and nose wounds
- The different drugs that would be available on the battlefield
- What purpose each drug has and when it should be used and for what condition

One of the most humorous things that happened was in one of the early classes. The instructor was discussing evolution and how we had all evolved from other animals. So he used an example to prove his point. He said that in a group of approximately fifty men, he could prove that one in an average of fifty would show how we are related to other species. There were only about thirty-five to forty in the class so he said that possibly his example would not show up today. But he wanted to try anyway. He asked everyone to stand up and take off their tee shirts (we all had on tee shirts and shorts). Then we were to pull our shorts a couple of inches below our belly button. We were told to look at each other and see if one of us had a series of nipples. He said that all of us have one set, but one out of fifty men has a series of three to sometimes four sets of nipples. He said if we have them we may have thought they were moles but they are not! The extra nipples demonstrate that we are evolved from other species and the correlation between male and female. Now look! We all looked at each other, and lo and behold one fellow had three sets of nipples above his shorts! We were all amazed and stared at this guy. The instructor had him come up in front of the class so everyone could see him. The instructor then said, "See, I told you. We all are evolved from other animals. Evolution is true. There is no God. Don't you all agree? Raise your hand if you do." Reluctantly a few did. I, of course, did not! It was interesting, and the poor guy with all the nipples was really embarrassed. This example was interesting; but does it prove evolution? Some time when there are a group of fifty guys, try this. It was interesting and did make me think! Also, if fifty women exposed themselves the same topless way, one woman would have multiple nipples? That would be a lot more interesting to see!

We were then tested essentially on what we remembered in med I. After two weeks we graduated to med II. Those with low grades were rushed to Korea. The rest of us went on to med II. At that time in Korea there were a higher percentage of medics and officers who were being killed than regular army soldiers, so they needed medics very badly. There were so many being killed that they no longer wore Red Cross emblems and officers no longer wore pins with their rank. They then melted in with the rest of the soldiers.

MED II

Med II was more intense with more battlefield situations. It was a true battlefield atmosphere at all times. We gave blood, took blood, and gave intravenous feedings. We practiced all types of battlefield emergencies. We were shown how to treat the patients with the worst or most severe injuries first. We learned all the possible dos and don'ts in typical battlefield conditions. Our instructors had great experience in battlefield conditions because they had all gone through WWII and they passed their knowledge on to all of us. By the end of med II, I was very relaxed and confident about my future as a medic going overseas into any battlefield situations.

WEEKEND BREAK TO MEXICO

After med II, we had a long weekend break. So about ten of us who had never been to Mexico decided to take a bus to Nuevo Laredo, Mexico. This was the closest town in Mexico and was less than a half day from San Antonio, Texas. The main reason most servicemen went to the nearest town in Mexico was to visit cheap houses of prostitution in the red-light district of each town. Supposedly, all of us wanted to see what a village in Mexico was like and, of course, buy gifts for our families back home. We left on a Friday afternoon about 3:00 p.m. and arrived in Mexico in the early evening about 7:30 p.m. We first went through customs and then found a beautiful hotel right in the center of town to stay for two nights. We all shared a room with another med II graduate. All the rooms had private baths which was fantastic, and what a change from army latrines and showers. My partner was a shy, quiet, bookworm fellow from Sandusky, Ohio, named Virgil. I purposely picked Virgil because he was only interested in seeing Mexico and shopping for gifts for relatives. Some of the other guys definitely had other ideas and wanted just to see what the red-light district was like and to do nothing more. We found a great Mexican restaurant next door to the hotel and we all ate together. Dinner was really great and the food was really Tex-Mex, not pure Mexican, which was good. We finished dinner about 10:00 p.m. We all planned to meet for breakfast at 8:30 a.m., have breakfast, and then see the sights and shop. Virgil and I, like good boys, went to bed so we could be up and ready to go at 8:30. Some of the others were going to have beers and then come to bed. Everyone was excited. It was a new experience for all of us because none of us had ever been in another country before. Virgil and I were up and ready for breakfast. Only six of seven of our group arrived on time for breakfast. We were told by their roommates that the rest were sleeping and would catch up with us later. In the morning we toured the town, the churches, and anything historical. There was not a lot to see. This town for the previous three wars was the closest in Mexico for servicemen stationed in San Antonio to visit for various reasons. (My dad was in the Army Air Force in WWI and stationed at Kelly Field in San Antonio. He and his buddies had visited Mexico. He had forewarned me about Nuevo Laredo.) We shopped all afternoon. I bought Bev an alligator purse with a baby alligator attached to the outside of the front flap of the purse. In Mexico you barter for everything that you buy. They wanted $10.00 for the purse. I offered $2.00 and ended up paying $3.00. It was a steal and there was nothing like it in Minneapolis. I bought other small gifts for my mother, dad, and everyone else who I thought would appreciate something from Mexico. There were lots of great things that were all handmade and were very inexpensive. That night we all met again for a late dinner. After dinner we decided to find a Mexican place where there was Mexican music, singing, and a possible stage show. The waiter told us to hire a big taxi and the cab driver would know where to go that had that kind of atmosphere. So we did. This was our last night in Mexico and we wanted to make it special. By the way, no one drank anything but beer (and I hate beer) because it was the only thing that you could drink and not get sick with Montezuma's revenge! Boy, if someone got it they were sick for days. So all of us were feeling pretty high from all the beer we had been drinking. The cab driver spoke broken English and said there was just one place with music, singing, and a stage show but it was a long way away. It would cost $4.00 for the cab ride. So we all pitched in some money and we were on our way. The cab driver drove for miles and miles and it seemed like we were driving around in circles. Finally, there was a high wall and we could hear music playing. The driver drove to a road at the end of the wall and turned in there. All we could see were lights glowing and heard loud music playing by a Mexican band. We got out, paid the driver, and off he went. We all walked inside and it was obvious that this was not exactly what we expected. There was music, singing, and lots of half-nude women sitting on men's laps laughing and generally horsing around. We were the only servicemen in the place. Everyone else, male or female, was Mexican. It was a shock and a little scary.

We were in the middle of nowhere and in a pretty rough place with some really tough-looking people. We went to the bar and ordered a beer and then on came the women. Virgil and I said, "No, thanks," that we did not want company, but the rest of the guys were enjoying themselves. We guessed they had been to a similar place the night before or someplace else like this. Virgil and I decided to leave and find a taxi somewhere to get back to our hotel. We started walking but we had absolutely no idea where we were. At every house along the street women came out and offered themselves to us—from 50 cents to $1.00. They also said a lot of things I will not repeat. But guess where we ended up—in the red-light district. We then walked for about three more blocks and saw bright lights on the street behind the houses with all the women yelling at us. At the next corner we walked toward the lights and believe it or not we were on the street one block from our hotel. We were never farther than three or four blocks from our hotel after that long cab ride! Boy, were we taken to the cleaners and definitely set up, starting with the hotel waiter. The next morning we took a bus back to San Antonio to Fort Sam Houston and Brooke Army Hospital. What an educational weekend we had had but at least we did buy some nice gifts so it was not a total loss. One last comment, to my knowledge none of our group came down with the "clap." Sexually transmitted disease was pretty prevalent with servicemen coming back from Mexico.

Two weeks later I graduated to med III. Only the "best" got that far. There had been four training classes of med I, two training classes of med II, and now one class of med III.

MED III

Only about twenty-five of us were left after four training classes of med II. Everyone else was shipped to Korea or reassigned elsewhere. Practice really became intense. We had medical situation after situation in battlefield conditions daily and some at night. One nutty, funny thing occurred.

A mock battle was to be held with soldiers pretending to be our army and the others the enemy. We, the med III class, were invited to participate. We had created a medical bivouac near the Mexican border where the mock war was to be held. Snakes by the hundreds were everywhere. We pitched our tents in the wide open in spite of the temp being 110 degrees. The snakes liked the shade so we were told to stay away from under trees and shrubs.

During the night, while we were sitting around a campfire, a snake—a live, hissing rattler—was tied by its neck to a rope, and the rope then tied to a four-foot stick. The stick was passed around to see if someone was scared of snakes and would not take the stick. I cannot stand snakes and am frightened of them but I took the stick, laughed, and then passed it on. If someone would not touch the stick, he later had a dead snake thrown into his tent that night! We had a few medics and other corpsmen who had snakes thrown into their tents and into their bedrolls with them. The next day after breakfast we were all standing in formation waiting for assignments. The captain pointed to different soldiers and said, "You two are to be patients, you two carry the sick patients in a sling, and you two are medics at the operating station," and so forth. Four of us were left in the back row and the captain told us to disappear. So off we went with a deck of cards to a remote hilltop above a ravine. We were deep into a bridge game. About forty-five minutes later here came the commanding general of Fort Sam Houston with his staff, coming down the ravine reviewing the mock war. We saw them coming and we all lay flat on the ground of the hilltop so we would not be seen. We had our faces buried in the sand. Just then out came this wiggling little snake, about a foot long, slithering along just in front of me and the fellow next to me, Bruce. Bruce started to shake and make funny noises. I told him to hush and I tried cupping my hand over his mouth until the general and his staff were out of hearing range. Then Bruce said, "Pat, don't you know what kind of snake that is?" and I said no. He said that it was a coral snake, the deadliest small snake in the USA. I grabbed a big rock and crushed it! Oh, thank you, God! Oh, how I still hate snakes.

HOME

I still wrote Bev every day. My letters were a sure lot happier than from Fort Riley. Bev wrote back asking about my coming home soon on leave, about our forthcoming marriage, and how excited she was.

THE CITY OF SAN ANTONIO

San Antonio was a wonderful place to be stationed. I was able to see the Alamo and all the history surrounding the battle. San Antonio also has a fantastic zoo, one of the best in the country. The people in San Antonio were so nice to the servicemen. There have been army bases there since before WWI. My dad was in the Army Air Force stationed at Kelly Field during the First World War. All those years ago and they still liked army personnel.

LETTERMAN ARMY HOSPITAL, PRESIDIO OF SAN FRANCISCO, CALIFORNIA

Well, I graduated from med III and was then assigned to Letterman Army Hospital in San Francisco. I again was fortunate because my grades were so high that I was assigned to an army hospital in the USA rather than Korea.

LETTERMAN ARMY HOSPITAL

Letterman had been an army hospital since 1898. In 1911 it was named Letterman after Doctor Jonathan Letterman who was a major and the medical director of the Army of the Potomac. For many years it was the largest hospital in the USA. It was constructed in a quadrangle, most of it on one floor. There were a few other multilevel buildings attached and Letterman still had this layout during my time there.

But first, I had ten days furlough before reporting to Letterman. I drove straight home to Minneapolis with a friend from Brooke Army Hospital who was also from Minnesota. We drove straight through in his car.

WEDDING BELLS

Bev and I had a very small wedding in a Methodist church near Bev's home. It was a beautiful ceremony. Afterward we drove in my car that had been stored in my mother's garage to Chicago. We spent our wedding night in Wisconsin at a nice motel. We then drove on to Chicago and met my sister La Verne. La Verne had lived in Chicago for many years and was controller for Blue Cross Blue Shield at their corporate headquarters. She arranged a fabulous hotel for us and a beautiful dinner for two at a sensational restaurant. Then she arranged for us to see the play *Once upon a Mattress* with Carol Burnett before she became a movie and TV star. La Verne paid for everything—she was a very special sister.

We drove straight back to Minneapolis the following day. I hated to leave Bev after such a short but wonderful honeymoon but I had to get to San Francisco and it was nearly 2,000 miles away. I drove with another friend, Wayne, who was stationed at Letterman and on leave at home as well. We made the trip in three days with no car problems, even going through the desert in the heat of summer!

ARRIVAL AT LETTERMAN

Wayne had told me about Letterman and how beautiful the area was in the Presidio. The gorgeous shrubs, trees, and grounds were breathtaking. There were beautiful colonial-style homes that surrounded the hospital.

The main hospital was a sprawling, one-story, massive group of buildings all attached to each other. There were many other two- and three-story buildings around the main building which were all support units to the main hospital. I brought my orders to the army headquarters at the facility and reported to the master sergeant on duty. I was told where my barracks, the mess hall, theater, etc., were located. After what I had been through with basic training and medic training, this was like a resort. I then was told that I was assigned to S-1 and to report there tomorrow morning at 7:00 a.m. I was to report to a Captain Passage who was the head nurse at the ward and in charge of all personnel. I was shown a map as to where S-1 was. (It was a large two-story square block building, behind the main hospital.) Before leaving headquarters, I had asked exactly what the S-1 was and what would be my new assignment. I was told it was a large ward completely separated from the main hospital because it was for mental patients only.

I was then told it was a closed neuropsychiatric ward for war veterans who went "crazy" during the war in Korea. (Closed ward means only mentally ill patients, doctors, nurses, and medical corpsmen were allowed in the S-1. S-1 was not open to the public.) It was totally separated from the main hospital because of the type of patients residing there, as many were "nutcases" and could not be around other patients. He concluded by saying that it was a "nut house asylum" for only really crazy people! Well, you can imagine my expectations and the concept of working in S-1. I was very apprehensive to say the least. I had been rushed through three short-term medical schools in Texas expecting to be sent to Korea and there was never one class about mental illnesses or treatment of these conditions. I realized then that the classes' goal was to train medical corpsmen to treat battle casualties and to assist soldiers who had been shot or hurt in battle. But nary was a word said about any soldiers who had a nervous breakdown on the battlefield or went berserk during the war times. Well, I had a lot to learn in the coming months!

After I left the headquarters, I drove by the S-1 building to get my bearings. Try to imagine a building that is a square block in size. The main entrance to S-1 was directly behind the main hospital and across a street. When you are facing the entrance to S-1, on the street to the right of S-1 are tennis courts. Then directly behind S-1 was a street, and across the street is the headquarters for the MP's office. To the left side of the S-1 main entrance was another street with a two-story building which was part of the main hospital.

I went to my assigned living quarters, and what a difference from Brooke Hospital quarters and the "hellhole in Kansas." Here there were two corpsmen assigned to a room. We had closets and decent twin beds in each room. The johns or toilets were separate from the sinks, urinals, and showers, not everything wide open like my previous quarters. So we had a little privacy, a bit like home. It sure was a nice change. In fact, I was alone in my room at the time with no assigned roommate. The mess hall was also nice. It was set up like a cafeteria back home in Minneapolis. The food was excellent, and lots of it, and great desserts too! We had a free theater with first-run movies shown all the time. Plus, there were a whole series of buildings that said Psychiatric Open Ward. (The open wards were for patients nearly ready to return to duty or to be discharged from service.)

Well, the next morning I was up at 5:00 a.m., showered, used the private stalls, and dressed. I had been issued the uniforms that all medical corpsmen wore. They were called "whites"—four sets of pants that tied and four white jackets or coats that buttoned. I went to breakfast and then walked about a mile from the barracks to S-1. These were right on the San Francisco Bay. (Today probably the most expensive property in San Francisco bay area.)

MY ARRIVAL AT S-1

I went in the front door of S-1 into a reception room. A heavy metal door with barred window was directly in front of me. A big arm or handle was the lever to open the door to the inside. There were offices on the left and right. In the office on the right the lights were not on as yet. I would find out later that this was the office of three stenographers. Their jobs were to type case histories and then fill in or update information on patients that the doctors and nurses gave to them. To my left was an office with a large desk and a sergeant seated behind it. There was a couch facing him with a corpsman in whites sitting there. To the sergeant's left was another office with the light also not on. I would find out later that this was the office of Red, the secretary to the only psychiatrist at S-1, Colonel Later. He was in charge of S-1 and the open ward. I told the sergeant who I was and he said that he had been expecting me. He said he was the sergeant who worked directly under Captain Passage and he was in charge of everything in the closed ward. He was not dressed in whites, probably trying to show his authority with all his stripes, etc. He then said that I was to take orders from him and no one else. He gave me his name as Master Sergeant O'Neill. He said he had been in the army eighteen years and knew everything and everybody of importance. He phoned inside to Captain Passage's office announcing my arrival. A few minutes later the captain came to the barred door. Sergeant O'Neill let her out and closed the door. He stopped and explained to me that no one but a trained corpsman was allowed to open the door to the inside. It was called "the door" and that I was not to forget it. No doctor or nurse or civilian employees who worked on the ward could touch the door that only authorized trained medical corpsmen were permitted to open it. Then he showed me the proper way to open the door. "The door" opened to the left. The trained corpsman or medic was to use his left hand and arm to pull the door lever down. The corpsman had to have his body blocking the entrance so that no patient could escape from the inside closed ward. I was to never open with my right hand or arm because a patient could hit the door, knocking it open, and escape. This had happened only once in past years and now under his authority it would never happen again. Any corpsman not following his instructions would be sent to jail and prosecuted for assisting a patient's escape. He asked if I completely understood. I said, "Yes, sir." He loved the homage.

I noticed that Captain Passage looked at him with a look of complete disdain. She then looked at me and I saluted her. The captain saluted me back and said it was not necessary on the ward to salute but thanked me anyway. She shook my hand and welcomed me to S-1. She then asked me to come inside and said that she would show me around the ward. The sergeant wanted to come with us but the captain said it was not necessary. He then opened "the door" for us and we went inside.

INSIDE S-1

Captain Passage was a very attractive, stately woman, about thirty-five, pretty, with a very warm and friendly face. She said that I was the fifth draftee assigned to the ward and she was anxious to get more draftees assigned and send some of the regular army personal elsewhere. She said many of them had been at S-1 too long and were becoming more like patients than medical corpsmen. She told me about everything going on with the patients and described the ward on the inside.

FIRST FLOOR

The first area was the barbershop. She introduced me to the two barbers whose nicknames were Frick and Frack. I never did know their real names. Frick and Frack were civilian employees. As it turned out, they were great guys—but more about them later.

Then we entered a large visiting room where relatives of patients could come for two hours a day in the evening to visit the patients. There were nice tables and chairs throughout the room.

The kitchen and dining room came next and it was a very neat layout with most of the tables like outdoor picnic tables with the benches attached. There were also some tables and chairs for up to four people. All the tables were attached to the floor. The cafeteria-style kitchen food smelled great. There were a few patients eating with some corpsmen in the room. Captain Passage introduced me to the medics and the patients there and said I would get to know everyone later.

The doctors' offices came next. They consisted of three individual offices with desks, chairs, file cabinets, etc. No doctors were at work yet.

We then entered the nurses' section. It had a high counter with desks behind for up to six nurses' stations. Two nurses were there and I met them both.

Captain Passage's office and an adjoining secretary office were next. Captain Passages' secretary was Corporal Sven S. from Minnesota. Sven and I became great friends as we were both from Minnesota.

Following along, we entered the women's section. These were individual rooms, some for one woman and some for two women. There was space for up to twenty to thirty patients in this section. At that time they had twenty-one women. The women patients were mostly dependents of servicemen from the army and air force. There were also some nurses, WACS and WAFS (Women's Auxiliary Ferrying Squadron) who were patients. The captain repeated that the patients were mostly dependents of servicemen. There was also a nurses' station in the women's section with desks for three nurses and bathrooms and shower rooms for the patients. Then Captain Passage opened a door to an outside space which was quite large, with metal mesh walls about twelve feet high. This area faced the MP's station across the street.

When the women patients were outside, they could wave at the MPs or anyone walking along the sidewalk. We then went into a large room for patients to play cards, relax to music, and exercise.

Next we came to the seclusion rooms. There were two on each floor. These rooms had padded walls and cushioned floors for violent patients to calm down after they had become violent for some reason. There were no beds or furniture in these rooms.

There were two large elevators at the end of the hall that would hold a gurney or two and people. Then we came to staircases going up and staircases going down.

We walked down to the lower level (sounds better than basement). This was the play area and physical rehab for male patients only. There were two ping-pong tables, four card tables, one shuffle board with bags, and some very simple exercise equipment. Also they had two tables to mold clay or create paintings. The outside door led to a big outside basketball courtyard at least two stories high. On top of the fence were rolls of barbed wire attached to the top of the fence. It would be nearly impossible for a patient to climb out. Two army nurses, who surprisingly were twin sisters, were in charge. These were both two absolutely beautiful ladies, one more beautiful than the other—if you could tell them apart. They were natural redheads with the prettiest freckles and very well endowed. One interesting tidbit is that the army does not allow fraternizing between officers and non-coms or regular GIs. But if I had not been recently married to Bev, who was very beautiful, it might have been worth the risk!

SECOND FLOOR: TREATMENT ROOMS—TWO TYPES OF TREATMENT

Captain explained at length that there are two types of treatment for mental illness at this facility. The first was electroconvulsive treatments. This shock treatment was called ECT. These treatments were started in the eighteenth century. (Old Ben Franklin actually experimented with shock treatments on himself!) It was and is mainly used for psychotic or paranoid schizophrenia or very violent patients—patients with aggressive behavior or who are catatonic. First the patient was strapped face up to a gurney, a movable high bed. The nurse then checked the patient's blood pressure and heart rate. If everything was normal or satisfactory, the treatment began. The patient was usually given a mild anesthesia or muscle relaxer. A medic was on each side holding down the patient's shoulders solidly against the bed. A nurse put a tongue depressor in his or her mouth between their teeth. This was so the patient did not bite their tongue. In the past during the procedure some patients had actually bitten their tongue off. In some cases, a third medic lay over the top of the patient's legs to hold them in place. Then an oily substance like Vaseline was put on the each side of the patient's temple. Electrodes from the ECT machine were then applied to the two Vaseline areas by a doctor (in some instances this was done by a nurse with training). This was called a bilateral procedure. A specific voltage of 800 milliamps and several hundred watts was set and the electric switch was turned on for up to six seconds. Then the switch is turned off. The patient has a "grand mal seizure" which is like an epileptic seizure. He or she shakes unbelievably and then becomes rigid throughout their entire body. Their eyes bulge out and they make horrible screeching sounds. She said that the time would seem like it was an hour but in reality it is only about thirty seconds that this seizure is occurring. The patient is then comatose, totally relaxed and out of it. The patient was then wheeled into a recovery room and moved to bed. The patient then sleeps for up to two hours. He or she does not remember anything about the ECT treatment. This bothered many patients because they do not remember one thing that really happened during the treatment and they feel very lost and confused.

She continued that he or she was then taken to breakfast sometimes in a wheelchair and are then fed. If they cannot feed themselves; the medic was to feed them. The medic stays with them at all times. Most patients receive a series of six treatments but there have been cases of patients having hundreds. She further explained that these ECT treatment shocks or jumpstarts the brain causing neurotransmissions. It has been found that ECT helps temporarily in about 80 percent of the cases. But in about six months the patient may have a relapse. Captain Passage said that there was another procedure that was sometimes done in some public mental institutions. In these they perform an actual lobotomy. A lobotomy is the surgical removal of one or more of the patient's cerebral nerve tracts. In theory this treatment is doing what ECT does but is a much more severe treatment. (But in my research I found that the records show that the army did not believe in or have ever performed lobotomy treatments.)

The second type of treatment was the deep insulin therapy. Captain Passage took me into the deep insulin therapy room. This type of treatment started in 1936 and has been used effectively since then in army hospitals. Heavy doses of insulin as high as 450 units but usually 100 to 150 units of insulin are given to a patient. This insulin reduces the blood sugar in the body and creates a coma for up to four to six hours. What happens is the procedure blocks the nerve cells and then strengthens and restores the nerve cells, causing hopefully the recovery of the patient. The patient must be watched and monitored very closely during this time because it is possible for a patient to die before recovery. Some insulin therapy cannot be reversed. The captain said that this must help glycemia control. The treatment was usually for a minimum of five days in a row, and up to fifty to sixty comas was the maximum. The patient may benefit with considerably less that fifty to sixty comas. Also seizures can happen during these comas. The patient may vomit or have incontinence during comas. Sometimes on a patient's day off from insulin therapy, they will be given ECT. The danger of shock has to be really monitored.

She said that the best candidates for these insulin treatments are patients who are psychotic or have schizophrenia (the inability to understand whether things in their environment are real or not).

MOVING TO THE PRISONER SECTION

This prisoner section wing was off limits to other patients. Only doctors, nurses, or medics were allowed into this section. The patient's food was brought to them and they were confined to this section exclusively except for therapy or medical and dental appointments in the main hospital. Rarely a patient who was a minor criminal would be allowed in a recreation area and then only with supervision. Patients who were murderers, rapists, thieves, patients for potential murders, kleptomaniacs (stealing), pyromania patients (starting fires), and AWOL patients (soldiers who tried to leave the army without permission or retreated without orders in battle) were in this section. This section was limited to fifteen patients. Captain Passage said that Colonel Later, who was in charge of S-1 and the open ward, took care of the most severe cases. None of the other doctors were psychiatrists except the Colonel.

GENERAL INFORMATION

The captain also told me to notice that all S-1 patients wore maroon drawstring pants and Ike jackets (jackets that were waist high in length) and slippers. All medical patients in all the wards, except the closed psychiatric ward S-1, wore blue pants and blue Ike jackets. The reason for this clothes color difference was so when mental patients were outside S-1 for dental or medical appointments it was very obvious to identify them at all times. Also, most other medical patients and most personnel were afraid of S-1 patients. The captain said that most of our patients had a mental disease and were harmless.

MY FIRST ASSIGNMENT AT S-1

After Captain Passage had toured the building and explained everything to me, I was assigned by Master Sergeant O'Neill to assist in performing an ECT. I found out later that this was the lowest starting job at S-1. There were only a few tasks below this position which I also discovered very quickly.

Fortunately, Captain Passage had explained about ECT and the rules that were the medic's responsibilities to perform. The first patient was about twenty-three years old and very frightened because this would be his first treatment. The nurse took his blood pressure and heart rate. She then gave him a shot of either a muscle relaxer or anesthesia. The nurse then told me to hold down the patient's right shoulder using the lower part of my left arm and with my weight shifted to that position and softly pressing on his shoulder. Another medic was doing the same on the patient's left shoulder. A third medic lay across the legs of the patient. Vaseline was applied to both temples of the patient's head. Then the doctor applied the electrodes and hit the switch. It was unbelievable—much worse than the captain had described. I guess unless you have seen this treatment, it is indescribable! The patient's body leaped in the air maybe six inches. He started to shake all over and became as rigid as a solid rock. He was rocking up and down and was nearly impossible to hold down. Then these horrible noises came out of his mouth, near screams like nothing I have heard before, and he started frothing at the mouth. Then it all stopped! He totally collapsed and was completely relaxed. The tongue depressor and the restraints were removed. He was covered with a sheet and taken into a recovery room and moved to a bed. A nurse was there at all times monitoring his rest and eventual recovery. (In the past I had seen two or three people on the street having epileptic seizures, but nothing like this.)

A doctor later told me that many of the patients who were manic-depressive, violent, catatonic, or schizophrenic were the best candidates for ECT.

Well, that was my first patient. But by the end of the first day I had held down nearly fifty patients for ECTs. Each treatment took about seven to eight minutes. We worked giving treatments on various patients all morning for about four hours. We then had a break for half hour to eat lunch and then back to the ECT room for another three hours. (If my memory is correct, we performed ECT on about forty-seven or forty-eight patients that first day.) We had a few women, two prisoners, and the balance were regular patients. In the afternoon a different doctor and nurse worked in the treatment room. But the same two other medical corpsmen and I from the morning shift stayed on in the ECT room and worked all day. We did switch around positions during the day. I became an expert at all three. We were all draftees and all new to the ward in the past week. We were the lowest on the pecking order on the ward. The half-hour lunch break was a relief but I could not eat anything then or at dinner that night. This important job went on for three days.

MEDICAL TEAM VISITED ECT ROOM

My third day there we had a visiting group of three doctors and three nurses watch the treatments being performed. None of them had ever witnessed an ECT procedure before. After two patients had completed their treatments, one nurse fainted and one doctor vomited all over the place. (Guess who cleaned up the vomit—the lowest person on the totem pole!) There are worse jobs than being a medic in the ECT room, but at that time I could not think of any! During this time I never vomited but I could not eat much for some time and had trouble sleeping because of my horrible dreams about the treatments. The atmosphere inside S-1 definitely affected a normal person working inside the ward.

I would learn in time that the treatments definitely helped some of the patients who were violent, catatonic, or depressed. But the many of the patients showed no improvement at all. I would also learn that if even quiet, nonviolent patients are mistreated by personnel on the ward, they became like animals.

INCIDENTS IN THE SNAKE PIT

On the fourth day I was assigned to bring patients down to the dining room for breakfast and assist in feeding some of the patients. That day one patient in the dining room became violent. He started screaming and said his food was full of worms and bugs and threw his plate, hitting a regular army medic. No harm was done to the medic except that he got some eggs on his whites. But the medic and another old-time regular army medic grabbed the little fellow, hit him in the stomach very hard, and threw him to the ground while another old medic brought a straightjacket. I helped put the jacket on the patient. They gave the patient a shot to knock him out. I was totally shocked and horrified by the patient being beaten for such a minor infraction. (This was my first of many incidents of this type.) The patient was then taken to a seclusion room and the door was closed. Then two of the regular army medics (one was the one who was hit by the food) started to kick and beat the patient ferociously—but not on his face where it would be obvious. They all laughed and said they always do this to these dumbbells. Then they said that these jerks deserve the beatings and never remember it happening. I was completely horrified as I had never seen anything like this before in my life! Please remember this was only my fourth day at S-1 and I was new to things like this happening. I then said to the corpsmen who did the beating that this was totally wrong to hit any really harmless person who is ill, and I would not allow it to happen again in my presence. I said for them to stop beating the patient now or they would have to fight me along with the patient! I also said that I would report this to Captain Passage. They laughed and said that they never do it when she is around or nearby but she wouldn't do anything about it because she needed them to run the place. They said that I had best go along with the way they ran things or else. But they did stop beating any disturbed patients around me. But I was now an outsider to the regular army "clique." They must have said something to their buddy Sergeant O'Neill because he kept giving me every dirty job to do. I really think he was hoping I would ask to be transferred to the main hospital. Some examples of this were if a patient was to vomit all over himself and on the floor or a patient was put into a seclusion room and masturbated all over himself and then rubbed it on the walls, I had to clean it up. Each time I was always ordered by Sergeant O'Neill to clean up the mess and also the patient. I never complained but did as I was ordered. It was not a very pleasant life in S-1 at that time. They, the "clique," did stop mistreating patients most of the time when I was on duty or nearby. But I only worked one shift and there were two shifts each day. So many violent incidents to patients continued on other shifts or at night or on my days off. I was told by other draftees and civilian personnel about patients being beaten and abused when I was absent. Many of the other draftees respected me for my position and so did the civilian employees who did lots of the dirty work on the ward before I arrived. After my first incident happened and everyone found out about it, a few of the other draftees started to also stand up to the "clique." I still had the dirty jobs assigned to me by the sergeant that the civilian employees used to have of cleaning up patients who had made a mess on themselves on the ward. All the civilian employees were black, Hispanic, or Chinese. They were all treated pretty badly by the "clique" and were like slaves to the "clique." It was a terrible atmosphere at all times. Everything really awful a person has ever heard about some horrible state hospitals was happening at S-1.

The mistreating of patients had been going on for long before I arrived. It had created a mad house in the ward. Patients were constantly fighting with each other. Also, some were trying to escape through "the door." And when upset, some butted their heads against the walls in the corridors. It was general mayhem. The emergencies seemed hourly. The emergency bell would ring, sending the medics to the lower level, to the second floor, and to the dining room to assist in solving the dilemmas. Many of the problems were caused by the "clique" group taunting a patient or teasing the patients into a frenzy. The "clique" thought this was funny because they said the patients were stupid animals and should be treated the same. It was terrible all the time, totally out of control. Even a few of the nurses began to dislike the patients. Why? Because as time progressed some of the patients became bolder as they were treated like wild animals and they began to act the same. A nurse or two were being fondled by patients and one nurse even got slapped in the face. The patient said that the nurse was a bad little girl. This particular nurse weighed about 220 pounds and was six feet tall. She slapped him back. He cried, " Mommy, Mommy, don't hit me." Many times the "clique" caused these things to occur. They would tell a patient that a nurse was in love with him and he should go kiss her or pat her fanny. Some listened and thought it was true and would do what the "clique" suggested, then the "clique" would just laugh and laugh. I have to admit some things were laughable but pitiful at the same time. I, being new and an outsider, could not do too much about these situations. I and a few other draftees did say to the "clique" to stop teasing the patients. I believe it did stop patients from being beaten as often by the "clique." Normally these situations would happen in the late afternoon or early evening. Patients seemed to get upset just before dinner. Sometimes minor incidents flared up while waiting for the cafeteria to open. One patient would push another or push ahead in line of another patient, "bucking the old chow line." A minor fight would start but if you said, "Stop or no dinner," that usually worked. But many times the "clique" would mix in to the foray and actually pick a fight with some meek little guy who had said nothing more than to please stay in line to another patient. The "clique" would then push the little guy or sometimes slap him on the face. They would tell him to shut up and then laughed.

Besides the beatings and the teasing, if a patient were to be slow in moving out of the way or standing catatonic, as many patients were, the "clique" just pushed them aside and in some cases just knocked them down.

Again, this never happened when the brass was around. And, of course, the patient was not in any shape to tell anyone. These "clique" members seldom picked on a big guy because they were not sure what he would do. Emergencies with patients happened sometimes hourly. It was rare when an emergency only occurred daily or a few times only twice a day. A patient who really went wild or berserk had the strength that was superhuman. I once saw a 130-pound little guy pick up a 200-pound medic and throw him against the wall. In some instances the "clique" had good reason to get mad or want to hit a sick patient but he did not. But this was rare. There were ways to subdue a violent person without doing harm to them. A patient with a sharp object, rarely a knife but more often they used items such as broken bottles or even a big salt shaker with the top broken creating a jagged raw edge would jab it at anyone or everyone. In most cases, bringing a twin-size mattress and pushing it into the disturbed patient would stop the frenzy. Some tough "clique" member would hit a patient or try to twist or break the patient's arm. They in turn would always say it was an accident.

Of course when two patients were in a fight, one would always end up getting beaten by the "clique" who were in the process of breaking up the fight. It was always supposedly not intentional, of course. This was what was happening at S-1 daily at that time. The "clique" also knew that many of the doctors who were assigned to the ward had absolutely no psychiatric background. These doctors had medical training but rarely had education on working with or about mental patients. During my stay at S-1, the only psychiatrist was Colonel Later, who was in charge of all the patients at S-1 and the open ward patients who were all down on the bay wards. In some cases the medics knew more about a particular patient's condition than the doctors. Certainly most of the nurses knew considerably more about each patient. The "clique" used this knowledge to their advantage. They would "kiss up" the doctors all the time! Please understand I am not against regular army personnel—many of them fought in WWII and many in Korea. But as a group they were crude, uneducated, overbearing egomaniacs who looked down at anyone who was not a veteran or regular army. (Some were nice people, particularly those at Brooke Army Hospital, but none that I met at Fort Riley. Here they wanted to create in only six weeks robots who would respond at an immediate call to action. And it worked.) I have to admit they did create in a short time a great group of draftee soldiers who were ready for anything and anybody. Those at Brooke Army Hospital were all fabulous people and respected everyone. This group at S-1, the "clique," as a whole was bored to death and thought it was fun harassing the inmates of the asylum. It certainly was not a warm, caring atmosphere to help sick people who had serious problems. And most of the patients could be helped in time with proper treatment.

Two more instances occurred within the next week in my presence.

FIRST INCIDENT

The first incident was when a patient was pushed by a "clique" member. The patient was doing nothing but walking around depressed. The medic pushed him and said for him to get out of his way because he was busy. The patient pushed back real hard. The corpsman went nuts and hit the patient repeatedly in the stomach very hard. I was standing about ten feet away when this happened. The patient fell and was obviously hurt. I told the corpsman to stop this but the corpsman took a swing at me. I quickly hit his arm and tackled the jerk. He fell really hard. I flipped him over and got an armlock called a chicken wing on this jerk. I held him down and told him to calm down or else. I forced the chicken wing forward which hurt like hell. He said, "Okay, I quit." By the way, he outweighed me by many pounds of blubber.

ANOTHER INCIDENT

Another patient tried to escape out of "the door." He was screaming "Geronimo" at the top of his lungs and pounding on "the door." "The door" was not even open, but the patient did not know because he was completely out of it. I was inside the ward headed toward "the door" at the time and a "clique" non-com was ahead of me. He grabbed the patient, a little guy, around the neck in a choke hold. Actually it looked like he was trying to break the patient's neck. The patient was turning blue from a lack of oxygen. The bully had a big smile on his face. I said to let him go very loudly. The bully just laughed. So I gave him one hell of a kidney punch and then another one for good measure. Boy, did he quickly let go of the patient! He started screaming worse than the patient and he fell down crying. I have been hurt lots of times but never in the kidneys. I guess it really does hurt. The patient calmed down and the non-com went out into the sergeant's office. Nothing further was said to me by anyone.

MORE INCIDENTS WITH THE "CLIQUE"

Morry was a patient who had been in Korea during the Inchon Landing in September 1950. It was first thought that Morry had collapsed from combat fatigue. He was eventually sent to the 361st Station Hospital in Tokyo because he had developed severe mental problems and this hospital had a psychiatric department. He had become schizophrenic which meant he had no ability to know if things were real or not. He was given a series of ECTs in Tokyo and then forwarded to S-1. At S-1 he began his second round of ECT treatments. Between treatments he would curl up in a corner of a room or hallway corner and make all kinds of weird sounds while rocking back and forth. One afternoon Morry was in a first floor hallway corner doing "his thing" and one of the "clique" came by and said to Morry," Get up and stop your crap right now." Morry, being oblivious to anything going on around, just continued rocking and making noises. The corpsman kicked Morry real hard and said, "Get up now or the seclusion room for you." Morry, of course, did not move. The character kicked Morry three more times and called for help from another member of the "clique" to bring a straightjacket. So they put Morry in the jacket and dragged him to seclusion. This incident was witnessed by Huan Y. and another civilian worker. In the seclusion room nearby, they saw both guys kick Morry a few more times—laughing all the time. Afterward Morry had terrible bruises and a possible broken rib. The nurses asked what happened and the "clique" said Morry was violent and then had to be put into seclusion. They said he was throwing himself against the walls and pounding his own body. This was not very likely for a patient with schizophrenia with all the walls and floor heavily padded in the seclusion room.

Another time a patient, Dom M., kept trying to come into the insulin therapy room talking gibberish. Earlier in the day the patient had had an ECT treatment. He was hallucinating, drooling, and talking incoherently. The nurse called for medic assistance to remove the patient. Two of the "clique" came quickly and were dragging the little guy to a seclusion room. The little guy, Dom M., drooled on one of the "clique" medics and the medic screamed that the little SOB was spitting on him. He grabbed a towel from someplace on a table and jammed it into Dom's mouth with tremendous force. Dom started choking and tried to spit out the towel. The medic did not let up until Dom was in seclusion. He then put part of the towel over Dom's nostrils so he could not breathe. Dom was *turning blue*! Another medic told the stupid medic to stop because he was killing him. He finally did and pulled the towel out of Dom's mouth. The nurse did not see this as she could not leave the insulin therapy room, but it was seen again by a civilian employee who told me.

VIOLENT PATIENT AND THE "CLIQUE"

One day a patient, Bobby, was coming down the stairs and accidentally fell and accidentally pushed the patient ahead of him down the stairs. The pushed patient—a really big guy, Jesse—got very angry and hit Bobby in the mouth, causing his mouth to bleed. A nurse seeing the fight called the med office for help. Medical corpsmen at once were sent to the scene on the first floor. Two of the "clique" arrived first and were trying to control

Jesse unsuccessfully. I arrived just as Jesse hauled off and hit one of the "cliques" in the stomach, so they started hitting back. I yelled stop and Jesse did as well, but the guy was enraged and did not. Jesse went down. We got a straightjacket on him quickly. He was taken to seclusion. I went along so no one would hit Jesse again. The "clique" corpsmen both looked at me and grumbled but did nothing more. The nurse did report the incident to Captain Passage. The two medics were called down for hitting a patient. But because the patient hit first, they were not accused of anything. Captain Passage did have them transferred from S-1 to the main hospital for duty. In this incident I could see why the one medic hit back, because it was natural reflex, but there was no reason for the other medic to keep on hitting Jesse over and over.

ONGOING PROBLEMS WITH THE "CLIQUE"

A problem ongoing with the "clique" was the daily abuse of all the catatonic, delusional, or paranoid patients. The "clique" thought it was really fun to constantly tease, slap, trip, or just push these incoherent patients. They knew the patient would never be able to report these daily incidents and would never strike back, with a few exceptions. In many cases the patient involved would become more upset but no one was aware of what caused the patient's agitation. Ninety-nine percent of these incidents were never seen by nurses, doctors, or even other medics. When finally the entire "clique" was transferred from S-1, this stopped completely. The patients became much more relaxed and calm.

ONE MORE INCIDENT WITH THE "CLIQUE" BEFORE THEY LEFT S-1

We had a new patient who was an air force war hero who had been flying over in Korea. Lieutenant Willie O. was flying his jet over North Korea and his plane was shot down. He was able to jump out before the jet crashed but as he was parachuting to the ground he was shot in the leg by a Korean sniper. The wound was not severe and he was able to bandage the wound with his first-aid kit. The lieutenant then walked for a few miles through enemy lines to the South Korean territory and was found by a United Nations advance patrol. This all happened late in the day so it was near darkness when he was found. He was immediately flown to Japan for recovery. The stress from the event had changed him completely from an easygoing happy soul to a frightened, paranoid person who was afraid of everything and everybody around him. The doctors treating him at a Japanese hospital had little success. The lieutenant was now flown to S-1 for further diagnosis and treatment. He was going through deep insulin therapy and the treatment seemed to be working. He became calm, very quiet, but smiling occasionally. One of the "cliques" must have been bored or just full of the devil and one day he started teasing Willie. He really scared Willie with something he said or did. Well, Willie hauled off and hit the creep, knocking him out. Willie got on top of the jerk and hit him repeatedly. It took four of us to pull Willie off before he killed him. Willie was given a shot that knocked him out and then put into seclusion to calm down. After that the "clique" left Willie completely alone and I guess they had learned their lesson and wanted no part of First Lieutenant Willie O. Willie completed his series of therapy and was his original self again. A week later Willie was sent back to duty to train other pilots.

CAPTAIN PASSAGE AND ME

One day Captain Passage called me into her office and closed the door. She told me to sit down for a minute. She wanted to have talk with me about things. She said that she was aware of the beating of patients but her hands were tied. The incidents were happening when she was off the ward. She said she was not going to tolerate this sadistic treatment of patients much longer. She went on to say she had been observing my progress and my attitude and could not be more impressed. She was aware of how I felt about the patients and how they should be treated properly at all times. She was also aware I was being given every dirty job on the ward and asked me to just put up with it a short time longer, that things were going to happen to change the personnel on the ward. I said I could take it; but if in my presence the "clique" tried to manhandle a patient again, I would stop it and fight the group. I had no other choice. She said she would back me 100 percent because it would be a court-martial for any corpsman touching or physically striking a patient. Boy, I felt fantastic; I had the complete backing of my boss!

HOORAY! BIG CHANGES AT S1

About a week after my conversation with Captain Passage, she announced the following: that there would be three important changes on the ward.

First, we would be having an additional group of ten new medic draftees arriving at S-1 this week.

Second, all the great veteran regular Army medics were being transferred to new important assignments. The transfers would include Sergeant O'Neill, and his replacement would be forthcoming in the near future.

Third, that PFC Patrick Shaw under her direction would be temporarily assigned in charge of the medical corpsman personnel on the ward and in charge of the receiving and discharge of all new patients at the admittance outside office of ex-sergeant O'Neill. (This particular assignment was the job of a warrant officer or at the very least a master sergeant, and now a lowly PFC draftee got the job!)

MY NEW LIFE AT S-1

On my first day of my new job I thought a lot about being in the army and a lot of my own time that had been wasted. I decided that I had two choices for the rest of my time in the service:

1. I could float along with the tide and not rock any more boats. The bad guys were gone and it would now be a pretty good life at S-1. All the promotions in rank had been frozen. So I was going to now be making $64.00 per month for the rest of my time in service. Bev was with me now (sorry, I have been so busy talking about the mess at the ward that I have not mentioned that Bev, my dear wife, had arrived from Minneapolis). So I could just ride out the rest of my time at good old S-1, or...

2. I could make my time left in the army fly by faster at S-1 and really accomplish something good. I would try along with the help of the other draftees to make S-1 into a great rehabilitation facility for the patients and the staff. So that is what I decided to do! Also, I said a little prayer and asked for God's help.

THE HEAD LEAD MEDIC OFFICE

Picture this: My office was to the left as you entered the small main lobby or entrance to S-1. To the left of my new office was Red's office. Red, if you remember, was Colonel Later's secretary. The Colonel was "next to God" and was in charge of S-1 and the open ward down by the bay.

My job now consisted of the following:

1. Entering new patients into the ward. When a new patient arrived, his or her valuables along with his or her clothes were given to me to be

tagged and sent to the main hospital until the patient was discharged. We had a safe to keep the patient's tagged valuables in until the patient's clothes and valuables were sent to the main hospital. I then sent the patient along with one of our medics inside to have the patient remove his or her clothes. They were then body checked for hidden knives, glass, money, or razor blades, mainly hidden between the cheeks of their rear. Women attendants or nurses checked the women exactly the same way. You would be surprised what is found in a patient's personal areas—all the things I just mentioned and even more stuff! Their clothes were then brought out to my office to be sent with their valuables to headquarters.

2. When a patient was discharged, the reverse procedure occurred.

3. I scheduled the personnel on the ward their days off and on. Also, I made out job assignments each weekday. This included the civilian employees too. I would go over this with Captain Passage weekly.

4. Oh, I forgot! My first job every morning when I arrived at work at 7:00 a.m. was to change the buttons and put new removable buttons on Colonel Later's three new doctor's coats. Why three? Well, I found out when he, the colonel, was upset he ripped his coat open and then tore off the buttons. He did this only in the privacy of his office. He would close the door then scream loudly and then rip his coat open. He would then regain his composure, put on a new coat, open his door, and

go on with his business. I would find out later the reasons for his rages were usually that there had been a stupid decision made by one of the new untrained doctors by misdiagnosing a patient's treatment. The new doctor would order an ECT treatment or deep insulin therapy given and they should not have done this procedure for that particular patient's mental problem. Some days the colonel would need more than three coats. In time, I began to wonder if the patients were not the only sick people at S-1! Red was very helpful in calming the colonel. Occasionally, she would get a cool cloth and put it on his forehead, which seemed to help.

5. If there were emergencies on the ward such as a patient becoming violent, the system was that I was notified immediately. The information was buzzed to my office. In turn I would send help to the problem area. All medics were told to drop everything and head for the emergency unless they were assisting in a treatment room or recovery room or feeding a patient in the cafeteria.

6. All patients' appointments were handled by my office because it required a medic to accompany an S-1 patient. We could not have too many patient appointments at one time or the ward would be understaffed.

7. Many patients were allowed outside-ward activities. On these occasions usually only on weekends patients would attend baseball or football games. I was responsible to arrange these activities and

make sure that they were properly escorted by staff. Sometimes the patients were able to visit a museum but not often because it was too difficult to control their movements. They never were to see a movie because it would be so easy to have one escape during the movie in a dark theater.

EMPLOYEE HUAN

Huan, a civilian employee on the ward, was a Chinese young man of about thirty. It is difficult to tell age of Chinese; they all look very young. Huan was American but born of Chinese parents in San Francisco's Chinatown. Previously he had gone to college for three years. Huan had two desires. He wanted to be a doctor or to open his own restaurant. We had a lot in common because I, too, wanted to be a doctor. Neither of us came from wealthy parents who could afford to send us to medical school. Huan was very aware of the treatment that I was getting from the regular Army "clique" and particularly the sergeant. Before I came to S-1, all the dirty tasks that had been assigned to me had been assigned to him or some other civilian employee. He or someone must have said something to Captain Passage about the situation and how I had resisted the "clique" treatment of patients and how I was now assigned all the dirty jobs. I will tell you more about Huan later.

MY LIFE OUTSIDE OF S-1

Bev came to San Francisco about a month after I had arrived. I had found a garden apartment in the Sunset District of San Francisco. This was a lovely area of homes built in the '30s and one block from Golden Gate Park. Golden Gate Park runs east and west and is about one-half mile wide and many miles long. The park is a beautiful area of trees, shrubs, and nature. It has many paths to take a stroll. It ran from our apartment all the way to the ocean about a mile away. This area of San Francisco was far enough away from the Bay Area that we seldom had fog—just lots of sunshine. The apartment was the first floor rear entrance off the garden. In this area homes had no basement because of the sea level. There was a single-car garage in the front with a lovely three-bedroom home on the second floor. Our apartment had a living room/bedroom that looked out on the garden, a kitchen with a dinette area, a laundry room, bath and shower. The apartment came completely furnished for $65 per month. Please remember as a PFC I made exactly $64 per month. Bev got a job at the Federal Reserve Bank in San Francisco. She had worked at a Federal Reserve

Bank in Minneapolis and was able to get a recommendation and a transfer. She made $30 per week which really helped. But with less than a $200-month income we really had to budget. Our expenses were the car, food, rent, and miscellaneous items.

Above our apartment was a three-bedroom residence. It was rented to the new executive VP of Safeway Food Stores and his wife. They were a nice couple. The home was owned by a Filipino woman in her eighties. This woman had been in the Bataan Death March during WWII and had survived.

I drove back and forth to the Presidio—remember I had my yellow Ford convertible. I entered through the rear gate. It only required a passkey to enter and there was no guard at the gate. So I wore my whites back and forth to work at S-1. The only time I wore a uniform was for inspection once per month but Captain Passage got me excused most times because my job was critical to be at S-1 at all times.

Most weekends I was off duty and Bev and I would go down to see Bev's brother, Dick, and his family. They lived in Los Altos, about twenty-five miles south of San Francisco. They were wonderful to us. It was nice having family so close. I had not met them before moving to California. Dick was an automobile and truck expert. He sold automotive parts to big companies. That's another story that I will talk about soon.

Northern California was so very different from Minnesota, so Bev and I toured as much as possible.

WINCHESTER HOUSE

One trip was to the Winchester House, which was nearby. The house was first started being built in 1884 by Sarah Winchester. The house cost over $5,500,000 to build. (Imagine what it would cost today.) Her husband started and owned Winchester Rifle Company. After the death of her husband, Mrs. Winchester moved from Connecticut to California. The home she built had 160 rooms and hundreds of staircases to nowhere. Mrs. Winchester felt as long as she kept building staircases she would never die. Also, she kept building rooms and staircases to confuse the evil spirits. She built over 600 rooms and then would tear them down as fast as they were built, ending up with the 160 left today. Mrs. Winchester was very small in stature and many steps on the staircases were only two inches high. There was one staircase that had seven flights with forty-four steps, rising only nine feet, each step two inches high. This was called the Switchback Staircase.

Mrs. Winchester also had a séance room. This room was so ghosts of Indians could not find the room. She had created many winding hallways to this special room which was really a complete apartment. The guide pushed a button and a wall slid open into another apartment. We went into this apartment and the guide opened a floor-to-ceiling window that revealed only another staircase that led to even another room that went into the special séance room. Another staircase descended seven steps and then went up eleven steps. All very confusing but it really was quite interesting. If you are in California, the Winchester House is still there today.

GIANT SEQUOIA TREES OR SIERRA
REDWOODS

One day we crossed over through Marin County north of San Francisco into the area with the giant sequoia trees also called the Sierra Redwoods. There is absolutely nothing like these trees anywhere in the world. The trees are so big they are indescribable. Some of them are over 3,500 years old!

TASTES OF CALIFORNIA

Bev and I had never eaten artichokes before coming to California. We were not alone because at that time artichokes were not distributed all over the USA. Bev and I learned how to eat them and they became one of our favorite foods. Abalone steaks were also new to us. We had never even heard of this mussel that was first extracted from its shell, then pounded and seasoned. The "steaks" were grilled or fried. What a wonderful taste and delicacy. At that time they were not expensive and were found everywhere—not just at Fisherman's Wharf.

The big cocktail was a Moscow mule—made of vodka and ginger beer over ice. Vodka was cheap then because it was new to USA. A large bottle cost not much more than a six pack of cokes. On our budget vodka was about all we could afford for entertainment. We were not beer drinkers and besides beer cost a lot more than vodka.

HIGHWAY 1

The drive along Highway 1, the highway along the ocean from San Francisco to Los Angeles, was and still is a place of magnificent beauty. The scenery and the ocean are breathtaking. We often drove down to Half Moon Bay on special occasions. The quaintness of this area and the unbelievable food was and is something else. We did not have much money but there were so many things to see that were free. One of these sites was Seal Islands. It was another great place that was not far from our apartment. We would drive over and watch the seals for hours. Back then people were even allowed to feed the seals.

There is no place in the world like northern California.

AUTO THEFT

One Sunday morning I was leaving the apartment to go to S-1 to work. As I came out in front, my car was missing. The street was completely flat but I looked both ways thinking that I might have left it in overdrive and it had rolled away. Of course it had not rolled anywhere. Someone had stolen my pride and joy—my 1949 yellow Ford convertible! I went back inside and called the police. They said they would investigate and advise if any cars like mine had been found. I then called the hospital and told them what happened and I could not get into work. We called Dick and Bug, Dick's wife, and they drove up in two of their cars. They said if our car was not found soon that I could use one of their cars, a 1937 Plymouth Coupe. What great relatives!

About 3:00 p.m. that day the police called to say that my car had been found—but it had been wrecked! They thought what happened was that whoever stole the car had driven it down south of San Francisco into the mountains. Then they left the car temporarily, planning to come back and strip the car for parts as it was worth more in parts than the car by itself. They had left it in overdrive and the police said they thought the car rolled the 200 feet down a mountain and was totally smashed in a ravine. This was the typical way cars were stolen in this area. The police told us to go to the police pound to find what was left of our car. We all drove to the police pound. Well, the car looked awful and was totally destroyed. There was no possibility of repairing it. The windows had all been rolled down, the top had been left up but on the backseat was a man's raincoat. In the raincoat was a cleaning receipt with a name and telephone number on the slip plus the cleaner's address. We reported this to the police but they said that unless there was a dead body in the car they were not interested in investigating the information on the slip. They suggested if the raincoat fits one of us to get it cleaned and keep it. They also said there had been three cars stolen the same night before within two blocks of our apartment. One was even a police car parked in front of a deli and taken while the policeman was inside getting a cup of coffee. They ended by saying that car theft was the biggest crime in the area. I guess I had watched too much "Dragnet" on TV thinking the police would use the raincoat and cleaning slip as great clues. Oh, shucks, no dead bodies. By the way the raincoat was too small so we gave it to The Salvation Army.

NEW CAR

We were very fortunate because in California the insurance gave the high blue book price on replacing vehicles. The insurance check came within days of my filing a claim with no problems. We were using Bug's little old car during the interim while we were looking for a new or used car. Dick suggested a Studebaker. He had owned and driven one and said how great they were on gas mileage, no repairs were ever needed, and they never burned oil. (He kept eighty pounds of pressure in his cars tires! Dick said the ride was a little hard but never had to buy new tires in five years.) We saw an ad for a 1949 one-owner Studebaker convertible that was dark green. I love convertibles. So Dick, Bev, and I went to look at the car. The outside and inside looked fine, although nothing like my yellow Ford which I had kept spotless and waxed all the time. Dick, the auto expert, checked the car under the hood. He looked under the car—no rust. He started the car and gunned the motor. We both drove it and it seemed fine. Lastly, Dick took a piece of clear white paper and held it against the exhaust tail pipe while the car was running. There was no sign of exhaust fumes or any dark stuff on the paper. Dick declared the car *perfect*. So we bought it that same day. Now, let me tell you about this cute, little Studebaker convertible. A few days after I purchased it, I went for gas and checked the oil. Surprisingly it was down two quarts. I thought maybe Dick was wrong when he checked the oil stick. So I had the oil changed. The following week I went to buy gas and checked the oil. Again it was down over three quarts. By the middle of the next week I did not need gas but I checked the oil again and it was down four quarts this time! It only held five quarts! It was burning more oil than gas! So I started looking for a new car. Guess what? The local Ford dealer said that he was going to be putting his wife's car on the market. It was a 1950 lime green with lime-green-and-black leather (vinyl) interior. It was also a convertible with a continental kit (a spare tire encased in a metal cover, same color as the car attached to the back of the car). The car had 12,000 actual miles on the speedometer. She had only had the car eighteen months and loved the car. He said that she was reluctant to give it up but he got her a new 1952 convertible in red. The dealership took my Studebaker in trade. So I got rid of the oil burner. Dick was a little embarrassed about the Studebaker but took it well. I guess even experts are not always right.

BACK TO THE NEW S-1

Things were really starting to improve at S-1. One of the new draftees had been in medical school when he was drafted. While in school he had worked part-time at a neuropsychiatric hospital in Baltimore. His name was Joel. Captain Passage put him into the deep insulin therapy section and he loved it. Soon he was in charge and all the nurses listened to his advice. Joel was a brilliant young man and the insulin therapy room ran with great precision. Joel had one fault or possibly a habit. On his days off, he would drink an entire case of "Bud" beer by himself. But Bev really liked his dry sense of sarcasm or humor so she invited him over to our apartment about twice a month for dinner. He wasn't a big eater so it cost very little to feed him. But the case of beer wasn't cheap. He never showed outwardly that he was intoxicated but he just got sleepy. He stayed over quite a few times and slept on the couch in the living room section and we were in our twin bed in the back section. What you will do for friends!

MASTER SERGEANT MATHEWS

About two weeks after I was assigned to the lead medic office, a new master sergeant arrived back from Korea. He had been shot in his leg in battle and returned to duty in the USA after his recovery in Japan. He had been one of the medics the North Koreans were trying to kill. Master Sergeant Mathews had a very slight limp in his left leg that he would always have. He could not go back to the front line in combat even as a medic because of this limp. The head lead medic at S-1 was supposed to be a second lieutenant, a warrant officer, or master sergeant. So of course he was assigned over me. This was the army protocol way of running any facility, and S-1 was an army facility. I was just getting the hang of things when he arrived. On the first day after he had been briefed by Captain Passage, Sergeant Mathews called me aside to say that the captain had told him that S-1 had been a terrible mess with the previous master sergeant and his "clique" of soldiers. She said that the "clique" had all been reassigned and now things were running very smoothly under my direction and along with a bunch of smart draftees on the inside. The captain had appointed me in charge until a new second lieutenant, warrant officer, or master sergeant was assigned to this position. She discussed that all the medics on the ward were now draftees (six more had been assigned to S-1 in the last week). Captain Passage elaborated on me and why she had selected me. She also explained that I had the respect of everyone on the ward, both staff and patients, and I was responsible for much of the great improvement at S-1. Sergeant Mathews said that he would not change the situation and he would work closely with me. He also said that he told the Captain that he had all the war he wanted in Korea and WWII and he did not want any battles at S-1. He ended by saying that I would run the lead medic office and he would only help and observe. Sergeant Mathews also said that at this stage of his army career he wanted to enjoy life. From that moment on everything he said about letting me run the ward was true. God was watching over me and giving me a lot of help by a really nice guy. If all regular army medics had been like Sergeant Mathews when I came, S-1 would have been a great place for patients and personnel from the start.

THE WOMEN'S SECTION

Three times in my year and a half at S-1, different women patients thought they were pregnant and of course were not. One patient was a WAC—let's call her Samantha. She complained constantly that she had pain in her stomach. She craved peanut butter and crackers all the time. Samantha actually had her stomach swell up like she was nine months pregnant. She went into labor and then her water actually broke! Of course, she had no baby. She then thought someone had stolen her baby. She accused the nurses, other patients, everyone she saw on the ward. She was finally transferred to a VA hospital. When one patient, like Samantha, thought she was pregnant, three or four others would think they were also. Fortunately, none of the others ever had their tummies swell up like Samantha's. We had a lot of women wanting attention by imagining they were pregnant. Captain Passage told all of us that what happened to Samantha had happened many times before with mentally ill patients. The power of the human mind over matter is something very special.

One very interesting case in the women's section was a woman called Mandy. Mandy was the wife of a sergeant stationed in the army at the Presidio. Her husband's name was Hiram and he was just a little guy, about 130 pounds and five feet two. Well, Mandy jumped out of the second story window of their apartment near the Presidio. She broke both legs pretty badly. She had casts on both legs from her thighs all the way to her ankles. She was a big woman, probably 225 pounds at least, and five feet five inches tall. Mandy was placed in a private room near the inside entrance to the women's section so that everyone walking by could not help but see Mandy and Mandy see them. Mandy was on the ward for a few days and the doctor reduced her medication so she now was starting to communicate with everyone. She was also communicating with the light fixture in the middle of the ceiling in her room. She would say, "Hiram,(that was her husband's name), Hiram, what's you doing up in dat light fixture? Gets down here, ya'll, and give me some lovin'!" She knew it was a light fixture but kept repeating, "Hiram, I need some lovin'. My pussy needs you so badly and my titties needs you too. I ain't had any lovin' fo' months. Now gits down here, ya'll, and git outa that light fixture *now!*" She repeated this all day for two days. I do not know exactly what she said at night. But hopefully she was asleep or they sedated her. The third day she did not talk to Hiram in the light fixture anymore. One of the nurses asked if Hiram was still in the light fixture. She said, "What's you talkin' about? He ain't never been up there. It's a light fixture. Is you crazy? Don't youse know the difference?"

So after a few days Mandy was allowed to sit up slightly in bed. She then started calling out to any male medic or doctor who came by her open door. She would say, "Honey, why's don't youse come in her' and yah give me some lovin? My pussy is starved for your big thing! See, her' is my pussy." And she would throw her sheet back and expose herself. Then she would say, pointing to her big personal place, "Comes in her' and kisses my sweet pussy. It needs you so badly." Sometimes she would expose her really big breasts and say, "Honey, comes in her' and start kissin' my boobies. They needs you kissin' them so much." It was so funny and everyone heard about Mandy's antics and wanted to go by her room to see what she was doing. This was especially true of all the medics on the ward. After she was on the ward for a few days, Hiram was allowed to see her for a few minutes but only at a distance. He could never be in the room without a nurse present. But by then she was only interested in all the medics or doctors who came by her room. We lost Mandy after about a one month. She was transferred to a state hospital. There never was another female patient quite like Mandy. We all missed her after she left, especially the medics.

We had one other interesting gal in the women's section—Anne Sue. Anne Sue was an attractive, overseas nurse who had a nervous breakdown in Korea. She was sent first to a hospital in Japan and then to us at S-1. She was recuperating quite well after a week or so at S-1. So she was then allowed to be outside in the open-air area for women. This was the open area that is enclosed with the twelve-foot-high metal mesh fencing. Remember, the MP's offices were across the street facing this fenced open area. One day she was by herself supposedly reading a book seated on one of the metal-attached benches. She had been outside for about one-half hour and the phone rang at my desk. It was from the MP office across the street directly behind S-1 and the women's screened open area. The MP said that one of the women patients was outside and was doing a striptease dance, singing as she stripped. Well, I called the nurses' station in the women's section and told a nurse what was happening. The nurse or nurses went out to the area and there was Anne Sue completely naked. She just completed her dancing and striptease show. Across the street were at least twenty MPs who had watched her show for about twenty minutes. Of course, they never called me until Anne Sue had completed her performance. Maybe in another life Anne Sue had been a professional dancer and performer! Later one of the MPs told me that she had been really good and not a bad singer either—better than some strip joints he had paid to see a performance! Anne Sue was never allowed outside again by herself.

AIR FORCE RECRUITS

While I was stationed at S-1, the highest percentage of patients in and out of the hospital was the air force recruits. This was probably because we had numerous air force training facilities close to San Francisco. We did not have any army draftees or newly enlisted soldiers who had mental breakdowns—possibly because there was not any army training base close by. The air force recruits' histories or their patient records read mostly the same. They had been babied or coddled by their mothers or parents at home. Air force basic training was a shock and quite tough, plus no mother was there to hold their hands. They often snapped under the pressure of the intense training. Most of them were in their early twenties, some even younger. Many had wet their beds during training and got laughed at by the non-coms and other air force recruits. When they were reprimanded, they cried and also many urinated all over themselves. Most of them wanted one thing and that was to go home to their parents. Very few were ever given ECT or deep insulin therapy treatments because their conditions were not that severe. After a short time at S-1, most of them were discharged into the care of their parents. I often wondered where they are today and what their life is like.

PRISONER SECTION

Just like Captain Passage had told me on my first day at S-1, there was a mixture of murderers, rapists, thieves, and soldiers who cracked up and many went AWOL. But then there were a few very, very unusual cases.

One case was really unusual. His name was Art. Art was a good-looking young man of about twenty-six or twenty-seven from Mankato, Minnesota, not far from my home in Minneapolis. Art had joined the army about two years before and he was in the infantry. He was shipped to Korea in late 1950. One day his platoon was on patrol and checking out houses and buildings in this little town looking for snipers. Art saw a pregnant woman walking down the street and he started to chase her and then tried to kill her with his bayonet. He wounded her badly but his buddies stopped him before he killed her. Everyone thought he was cracking up because he had been without sleep for three days previously plus all the pressure of the war in Korea. The incident was reported to superior officers and the decision was made to send Art on leave to Japan for a few weeks. There he would be under the supervision of some doctors who could help him be relieved of some of his stress. While in Japan everything went well for a week. He was allowed to go "out on the town" on a weekend in Japan. Well, Art saw another pregnant woman walking down the street and tried to choke her to death. Someone called the MPs and stopped him before she was dead. Art told the MPs that she was the enemy and was trying to attack him. A few days later in a hospital in Japan he saw a pregnant nurse and tried to kill her as well. He tried to choke her to death just like he had the Japanese women. He was restrained and given drugs to control his emotions. Art was never prosecuted as he was ruled mentally ill. But he was then sent to the S-1 facility. Because he was very rational most of the time, he was one of the few prisoners who were ever allowed to go into the lower-level basketball outside court area for air and relaxation every other day. Of course he was always supervised when he was in the basketball court. Art was completely normal to talk to, very warm and friendly. He was a very good-looking, blond, blue-eyed Scandinavian and very rational, except when he saw any pregnant women. He was kept in the prisoner section because occasionally a patient's visitor would be pregnant and the doctors were afraid what might happen. Art underwent a series of ECT treatments. We never knew if it helped because he was sent right after the treatments to a state hospital in Minnesota.

ANOTHER VERY SAD CASE

A Lieutenant Stan S. was flown from Japan to S-1. For many months he had been in two hospitals in Japan and had had over one hundred ECT treatments. Unbelievable but true. You would think his brain would have been mush after all those treatments!

Here is the background of Lieutenant S.'s illness. His captain ordered the lieutenant to send his platoon of forty men up a hill occupied by at least 300 Chinese soldiers who were all in foxholes. The lieutenant said this would be complete suicide and his men would all be killed. Lieutenant S. was aware that the Chinese were deeply entrenched with machine guns and heavy fire power. The captain told the lieutenant that he would be relieved of his command and he would be court-marshaled if he did not obey. Lieutenant S. said, "No, I will not!" The captain then ordered the platoon himself up the hill and all forty were massacred. Lieutenant S. started screaming and grabbed the captain around his neck and tried to kill him. The lieutenant had to be restrained by five other men. Then Lieutenant S. went totally crazy. He screamed and hollered repeatedly and had to be sedated! He was sent to a mental ward in Japan and there he had over one hundred shock treatments. All those shock treatments did not stop his hysteria. The lieutenant tried numerous times to kill the medics on the wards in the hospitals in Japan thinking they were his captain. Finally, he became semi-catatonic, drooling constantly, and mumbling things about his men. Of course no discipline was given to the captain who created this horrible situation. When Lieutenant S. arrived at S-1, he was still very calm but semi-catatonic. The lieutenant was a very handsome, big, rugged, solid-muscled man, about thirty-five years old. As I said, he was very calm when he arrived but on the first day was put into a seclusion room after he started screaming on the ward. He would have screaming fits of anger and hit the walls with his head and fists. Then he would become very calm and sedate. He was given a series of ECT treatments at S-1 and became very quiet and peaceful for a while. So he was transferred to a single bedroom on the second floor. There he was allowed to walk the halls and seemed to be improving tremendously. He started talking to people and even smiled and seemed to become normal. But then one day a nurse went into his room by herself. (No nurses were ever allowed into a room with a possible violent patient without corpsmen or medics with them.) He was sitting on a bed reading a book. She sat down next to him and gently stroked his hand and talked to him calmly. She was going to give him a sedative. He looked at her and then *wham!* He hit her in the face, knocking her out. Then he started screaming! The medics rushed in, put him in a straightjacket, and placed him back in seclusion. He was on the ward about three more weeks and then sent to a state mental hospital. What a horrible example of the bad, bad things in war that happen to nice, good people. God bless Lieutenant S., wherever you are. You deserved a better life.

MONOPOLY AND JESUS

On the happy note, there was a patient named Harry who came to our ward very depressed, possibly a manic-depressive. Harry was given deep insulin therapy combined with ECT and overnight became the happiest, most joyful patient on the ward. He spent a lot of time in rehab with the twins (the twin sisters/nurses in charge of the rehab unit). He played the game Monopoly for hours and hours with anyone who would play. He won thousands of dollars and property. He then mentally became a philanthropist. Harry started giving Monopoly money to only the people he really liked. One day he came to the barred window in "the door" at the main entrance to S-1 and called out," Pat, Pat, please come to the window." So I did. Then he said, "Pat, I really like you and you have been so good to me at S-1." Then he told me, "Jesus says in the Bible to 'give away all your wealth to the poor and follow me.' So I am giving away all my wealth and property and I want you to have both from me because I know you are very poor." (He was right.) "Here is $20,000 in money (Monopoly money) and the deed to a home on Park Place. God and I bless you and if you need more money, I still have more left!" (I still have the money and card to this day!) A short time later he was released to his parents' care. Harry was a very special person. Wherever you are, you touched me.

ANOTHER WEIRD STORY — ALEX

Alex had been in the army cavalry for fifteen years during WWII and Korea. He was a non-com stationed in Korea. I have no idea why we had horses in Korea unless to pull supplies or cannons or (???). Anyway, one day Alex was supposedly cleaning out a stable or brushing horses. He took a fire hose and stuck it up the rear of a horse and then turned on the water. Well, we were told there was pandemonium in the stable. The poor horse went wild. Alex was a big man but I am sure it was not easy pushing that hose up the rear of the poor horse. Alex started yelling, "Hi ho, Silver, away." He kept yelling and howling, "Yippee-i-oh, git along little doggie, yippee-i-oh." They said it took four MPs to restrain him. I mean Alex, not the horse. Alex was first sent to Japan to a hospital for ECT treatments then to our S-1. Alex was calm most of the time. But one day he talked another patient who most of the time was semi-comatose and delusional to get down on all fours, and Alex rode him like a horse all around the first floor halls yelling, "Giddy up, giddy up." Of course, he was put into a seclusion room without his "horse" and given a shot to calm him and put him out. Alex received a series of ECT treatments. He calmed down and became pleasant, quiet, and cooperative. He never again tried riding patients and was sent to a state hospital in his home state of Louisiana.

AMBULANCE DUTY

Every medic corpsman at Letterman of any capacity had to serve ambulance duty every three months for one night from 6 p.m. to 6 a.m. The hospital already had regular medics whose assignment was ambulance duty for day work from 6 a.m. to 6 p.m. All other medics assigned to the hospital in some other capacity in some ward had to pull this night duty. Most times this duty was uneventful. Usually it just amounted to us picking up a drunken soldier who was hurt in a fight at some bar close to the Presidio. We would then bring him back to the emergency section. Sometimes two drunken soldiers got hurt in the same fight. On one occasion we had to pick up a wounded soldier flown back from Korea from one of the nearby air force bases. Another time it was a patient for S-1. But mostly we played cards, talked about sports, and/or kibitz about someone or something waiting for an emergency to occur. One night we helped deliver two babies—all in the same night! One was a boy and one a girl. I had helped deliver puppies once when I was twelve years old but I guarantee it was not the same. We did have a short course one afternoon at Brooke Hospital discussing the possibility of this happening and what to do and not do. I will not go into a minute-by-minute or blow-by-blow of both deliveries but both babies and mothers survived the ordeals. In both cases when we got to the homes, the babies were already on the way! One woman had already had her water break and the baby was actually being born as we entered. The other call came about three hours later after we had returned to Letterman. This mother's water had broken in the ambulance. We asked her to hold on, that we were just fifteen minutes from the hospital, but she could not. The little black baby just popped out. This was her fourth child and I guess the more you have the faster they come! I went to see both mothers and babies at the maternity section afterward. The one mother wanted to name her baby after me but then decided that a black baby should not have an Irish name like Patrick. As I look back now, ambulance duty was exciting and a great learning experience.

BACK TO S-1

The two barbers there were very special. We called them Frick and Frack! Their real names, I found out later, were Fred and Frank. They had lots of stories about the escapades in the barber chairs. Most of the patients were good but a medical corpsman had to be in the room with each patient while they were being shaved or having a haircut. They massaged each patient's shoulders to get them to relax in the chair. This worked miracles. Quite a few fell asleep in the chair and the barbers had a heck of a time waking them. Frick and Frack became bored because things were running so well on the ward. All they did was cut hair and shave patients (no patient was allowed to shave themselves). This was quite a change from previously when there was so much chaos. When the "clique" was at S-1, there were so many emergencies occurring all day every day that there was never a dull moment. Now things were quiet most of the time and all they did was cut hair and shave patients eight hours a day five days a week. So in their free time they decided to develop a special hair cream that would grow hair. Frick and Frack really believed that if they could perfect this cream they could become millionaires. They tried it on every patient and every medic who thought he was starting to lose his hair. They guaranteed that the stuff could not hurt anyone but would only help grow hair quickly. The stuff had a terrible odor. It smelled like motor oil and was a light-brown color. It must have had Quaker State Motor Oil in it or something similar. I even tried it. They poured it on your head and then they massaged it into your scalp. It tingled slightly; and when you inhaled the fumes, it sure cleared your sinuses! I came home that night and Bev met me at the door and asked, "What is that terrible smell?" I told her that it was my hair. Then I explained about the barbers' new hair-growing cream. Bev said it was the worst-smelling stuff and asked me to please wash it out now! I had to wash my hair twice to get the odor out. I never tried it again but many patients did have a treatment every day and in some cases a few that were bald or partially bald did grow new hair! Frick and Frack were still perfecting the cream when I was discharged. I never saw it on the market but maybe they are still trying to perfect it in some barbershop.

One interesting fact was that the barbers always shaved patients with a straight razor. No patient ever tried to steal a razor. I often was concerned some patients who were suicidal might try to grab or steal it, although none ever tried. But many patients did steal saltshakers, kitchen plastic knives, and other things on the ward.

DOCTORS

I have already told you about Colonel Later and his peculiarities and the reasons why he got so upset. We always had three doctors as well as the Colonel who were assigned to the closed ward. In my time at S-1 not many doctors had psychiatric backgrounds or had worked with mental patients. Most were fresh out of college and were very enthusiastic and willing to help patients but they really had no knowledge on mental disease. One doctor would diagnose a patient as a manic-depressive and then would start shock treatment. Then that doctor would be transferred out and a new doctor who just arrived at the hospital would treat the same patient and he would give a totally different prognosis and stop the ECT completely. In many other cases if a new doctor came to the ward and he did not know what to do for a patient, he would automatically recommend ECT. The secretaries would actually spot some of the mistakes in the diagnosis in typing the patient's new history at S-1. Most of the time they would pass the information on to Captain Passage who would nicely try to discuss the problem with the new doctor. Colonel Later would read the same reports and then go "nuts,", close his door, start screaming, and then rip the buttons off his white doctor's jacket. Many times he would bring the new doctor into his office again with the door closed and yell about the stupidity of the doctor. The next day the doctor involved would ask for a transfer and usually got it. The doctors came and went like the wind. Colonel Later wanted to handle all the patients himself and it drove him crazy that it was impossible because there were just too many patients for one doctor to handle. So he took only the worst cases. He also handled any patient who had worked in army intelligence. The government was so afraid secrets might leak out to the enemy. Red, Colonel Later's secretary, was fabulous in handling the Colonel's tension level and calming him down. She would have made a great psychiatrist herself. If it had not been for Red, the colonel probably would have had a nervous breakdown himself. His emotions improved tremendously after the "clique" was transferred out. There were so many less emergencies on the ward after Sergeant O'Neill and his boys were gone. The atmosphere was calm most of the time in the ward now because the "clique" was replaced with intelligent, concerned draftees in all the important positions. Also the colonel had become much calmer. Red said that even now every time the emergency bell rang, the colonel would close his door, sit in his chair, and put his head in his hands and sometimes even cry. He took the ward so seriously it was a very good or very bad part of his life! He was completely dedicated to his work. In the new S-1 he smiled occasionally and even laughed a few times. One day he called me into his office and said he was aware of how much more efficiently the ward had become now and the patients were a lot more relaxed too. Captain Passage and Red had told him that I had a lot to do with it. I was told to keep up the good work. He closed by saying that I was indispensable at S-1. Well, I was two feet off the ground, to say the least!

THE OPEN WARD

The doctor or doctors assigned to the open ward stayed much longer than at S-1. They spent quality time with each patient using medication and group therapy to communicate help to the men on the open ward. Open-ward patients were usually there for a short time and then went back to an army assignment or received their discharge from the army. But there were two patients who were assigned to the open ward who committed suicide. In both cases they were thought to have gone AWOL and in both cases they were found in different vacated buildings down by the bay. There were at least ten buildings that had been at one time either barracks or storage units that were now empty. One patient had slashed his wrists and was found dead. The other was found when I was on ambulance duty at about 8 p.m. one evening. Some soldiers who were out for a walk after dinner one night stopped and looked in a dirty window of one of the vacant buildings. They saw a man hanging from a rafter. They called the MPs who called us to bring our ambulance to the location. The patient had been hanging in the building for at least a week but no one knew that at the time. We arrived about five minutes after the call. The MPs had smashed in one of the doors and as we entered the building and they were cutting the rope attached to the patient's neck, the body fell and split wide open! The odor was horrendous and everyone started to vomit. We all went outside and called the morgue people who then came and picked up the body. It was a godsend that we did not have to pick up the body. Fortunately, on ambulance duty we only worked with people who were alive!

S-1 EX-PATIENTS WHO COMMITTED SUICIDE

There were two other incidents of S-1 patients discharged from service at Lettermen who were living by themselves in San Francisco who committed suicide. In both cases these patients had been released or discharged right out of the S-1 closed ward. The reasons that this could happen were that these patients either had no relatives to be responsible for them upon discharge or they were not capable of going back to active duty for one reason or another. It was also possible that there was no state mental hospital available to send them to in the home state. Therefore, they were then released or discharged right to the streets of San Francisco. Some of these men ended up in skid row but some lived a normal life. A few had stopped back at S-1 to say hello and talk about how well they were doing in civilian life. Unfortunately that was not true of all the ex- patients. It was very sad each time a patient who still had some mental problems was released from S-1 on their own recognizance. I used to say a little prayer for each one of these people.

PATIENTS OUTSIDE TRIPS

Male patients who were doing very well recuperating at the ward or patients ready to be released were allowed to go to outside events. The 49er football games were the favorite. The 49er management was wonderful giving great seats free to Letterman Hospital army veterans. One Sunday the 49ers were playing I believe the Chicago Bears at Kezar Stadium. We had a busload of twenty patients and four medics go to the game. The patients from S-1 were seated on the thirty-yard line in the first two rows on the 49er side of the stadium. There was another busload of medical patients from Letterman also seated with them. Remember S-1 patients wore maroon outfits and the regular medical patients at the hospital wore blue. The game was in the fourth quarter with about ten minutes left in the game. The Bears had the ball and their quarterback threw a pass to an end on about the 49er's forty-five-yard line. The end was racing down the field. "He's at the forty, he's at the thirty-five on his way to what looks like a touchdown." Just then Jerry, an S-1 patient, jumped out on the field just in front of the end and tried to tackle the end! I was watching this on our TV at home because it was my day off. I could not believe what was happening. I saw this person in a maroon outfit jump out of the stadium seats and onto the football field. It was an S-1 patient! The Chicago Bear's end slowed down and was tackled by a 49er defensive back. The crowd went crazy! All the players from both sides ran out onto the field. Jerry was still on the field watching all the commotion. The officials could not decide what to do. Finally after what seemed like an hour, the decision was made. It was a first down for the Bears on the 49er's thirty-three-yard line. The Bears scored a short time later. Nothing happened to Jerry accept harsh words from the referees and the S-1 medics at the game. The bus left a few minutes later to return to S-1. Jerry was elated for days and a hero of the ward. I found out later that Jerry had been a very good linebacker in high school. I wonder what Jerry is doing today? Maybe he went on to college and became a star linebacker or defensive back. But I never saw him or his name on TV.

ANOTHER REALLY WILD INCIDENT OCCURRED DURING A 49ER'S GAME BUT AT THE HOSPITAL THIS TIME

I was working at S-1 one Sunday during football season. At about 11:30 a.m., we had a bus leave to attend the big game with twenty patients and five medical corpsmen. With five medical corpsmen off the ward, we were shorthanded. The patients' visiting hour fortunately was from 7:00 p.m. to 8:00 p.m. that evening so there would be plenty of corpsmen on the ward at that time. It was about 1:00 p.m. and I was sitting behind my desk talking with a medic, Pete. Pete was sitting on a corner of my big desk facing the small lobby area and "the door." A patient, Ben, was behind the mesh screen ranting and raving that he should have been discharged two weeks ago. He went on and on and on and it seemed like he would never stop. Ben was a Korean War veteran who had a nervous break-down in battle. He had had ECT treatments and was doing very well. But now Ben was waiting for his medical discharge from service. He was a big guy, about six feet four, and weighed about 250. His discharge was delayed for some unknown reason, but that is the army…

Just than a new doctor recently assigned to the ward came through the open door into the reception lobby from the outside. He went directly to "the door" and opened the latch with his right hand. Remember no doctor or anyone but an experienced medic was to ever touch "the door." Well, Ben from inside the closed ward slammed "the door" wide open, knocking the doctor down. Pete, who had been sitting on my desk, jumped up and ran the few steps into the commotion. Ben saw Pete coming and hauled off and hit him in the jaw as hard as he could. The sound of Pete's jaw breaking was so loud! Ben's blow had cracked Pete's jaw badly.

Pete was knocked out cold. I rang the emergency bell and yelled into the phone, "Escaped S-1 patient! Come to the front office." Immediately another medic, Bobby, arrived. I slammed "the door." I told Bobby that he was in charge and I took off after Ben. Ben was confused as he ran outside. He did not know what to do or where to go. So he ran straight ahead and up a few steps into the main hospital. I was at least ten yards behind him. All this happened so quickly. He went through the hospital door, paused, turned left, and ran down a long corridor through various wards and TV rooms. The TV rooms were occupied with patients sitting in chairs and wheel-chairs in their blue outfits and a few medical corpsmen all watching the football game. Ben would slam open the double doors at each section between wards and I was in pursuit still maybe ten yards behind. He knocked over one patient in a wheelchair and continued on down the corridor through more wards. I kept yelling that there was an escaped S-1 patient. Finally a medical corpsman in one of the TV rooms jumped up after Ben ahead of me. Ben went through a door at the end of the corridor to the outside with the medic close behind. Ben slammed the door as he went out thinking it would stop anyone behind him. Now he was outside and went on running down the street behind the row of colonels' mansions. Just off the sidewalk were heavy wooden platforms about six feet long and three feet wide that was where their garbage cans were sitting. Out of breath, Ben stopped, knocked over the garbage cans and picked up the heavy wooden platform, slamming it over the head of the medic directly behind him. The medic went down and was knocked out cold with the platform on top of him. Ben freed himself from the mess and turned to keep running. But I tackled him. Down he went on his face on the sidewalk. I got a chicken-wing wrestling hold on him with my right arm on his right arm and held him face down on the sidewalk with my left arm on the back of his neck and shoulders. Ben screamed and screamed, "Pat, let me up now or I will kill you. Let me up now or I will kill you *and* your wife!" He said this over and over. (He had been on the ward quite some time and knew my name and that I was married.) He kept pleading for me to let him escape, saying, "Let me go or I will kill your wife and cut her into little pieces." He said, "You know when I will get out, I will get you and your wife. Let me go now!" People just kept walking past me coming from church I guess. I repeatedly asked these people to please call the MPs and have them bring a straightjacket for this man. I told them he was an escaped S-1 patient and to please help! I am sure it was a sight to see. It was a crazy scene for people walking by to see, me holding down Ben with Ben yelling and my yelling for help and a medical corpsman lying knocked out near us. It seemed like hours, probably was not over ten to fifteen minutes. The MPs finally arrived and an ambulance came to take the corpsman to the emergency section. Ben was put in a straightjacket still screaming at me. A medic from the ambulance put some stuff on Ben's face because he was bleeding and had abrasions on his face from my pushing his face into the sidewalk. The young medical corpsman finally regained consciousness and seemed okay. He was taken away by ambulance to the emergency ward. We brought Ben back to a seclusion room and he had a shot to knock him out. The rest of the day was uneventful at S-1. I was so glad it was all over. Two days later Ben was back at "the door" and quietly now saying so only I could hear, "Pat, remember what I said. I will kill your wife and cut her into little pieces." He repeated this over and over again except when nurses or doctors were around, and then he was the model patient awaiting his discharge. There was nothing I could do but wait. Finally after a week his discharge came. I sent over to security for his clothing and valuables. After he was dressed, he came out to my office to get his valuables and sign papers. Then just before he left, he said, "Pat, I really liked you and I had no intention of hurting you or your wife. You were so good to me in the hospital and I know it was your job and responsibility to catch me. If I had your job, I would have done the same thing as it was your duty as a soldier. You are pretty good for a little guy." He gave me a big hug and said "God bless you," and walked out the door, discharged and a free man. I never told Bev about what Ben had said until long after he was gone.

I have to admit that I was very concerned. But so goes the antics of S-1 during the Korean War. Sometimes S-1 was a battleground more like the Civil War —American against American.

PATIENT PRIVILEGES

Originally some patients who were down to the wire on being released were allowed special privileges, such as leaving the premises with their wife or just strolling around the grounds. These patients were going to be discharged into their families' care. In a few rare instances they were even allowed overnight stays at their nearby family home or apartment. Only one time did a patient run away. But he was found the next day sitting quietly on a park bench by himself. The experiment of overnight visitations stopped after that incident.

PERSONAL LIFE OUTSIDE OF S-1

A close friend whom I met while I was staying in a barracks by the bay before Bev arrived was Bill B. Bill was a draftee from Sacramento. He was in his last year of dental school when he was drafted. He was assigned to Letterman in the dental department and his wife, Susan, was arriving in a few days from Sacramento. He had come to Letterman a few days ahead of me and bunked in the next room. Bill had found an apartment near the Presidio. Bill and Susan had been married less than a year and were childhood sweethearts just like Bev and I. So we had a lot in common. They played bridge and Bev and I played bridge. They also played tennis as did we. They liked getting together for dinner with friends and so did we. Well, about a week after Susan came and they moved into their furnished apartment, they invited just me over for dinner because Bev had not arrived yet. Then Bill told me that they had also invited a college friend of Susan's over that same night for dinner and to play bridge. I said fine. Then Bill contacted me again and asked if I would pick up Susan's friend, Becky, at her apartment and take her home afterward. At first I agreed but then started thinking about it. How could I do this, and should I tell Bev or not tell Bev? It just was not a proper thing to do for a married man even as casual as it seemed. So I contacted Bill again and said I just could not do this because I was married and did not feel it was the right thing to do. So I explained that I would have to pass on their offer for dinner and bridge. Bill and Susan thought this was the funniest thing they had ever heard of in their life. Bill said when he told Susan that night at home they both rolled on the floor with laughter thinking about how conservative I was. They told the story to everyone. (California was sure a lot more liberal then Minnesota.)

When Bev arrived, we got together with Bill and Susan many times for dinner and bridge. Each time Bill had to retell the story and he embellished it a lot.

Along the same line, Bev had a married cousin who was about twenty years older than we were and lived in San Francisco. Their names were Margie and Boyd. Boyd had a custom cabinet business and was very successful. One Friday they invited us out to dinner at their yacht club in Marin County. It was a very fancy, snobbish sort of place. While we were eating dinner, they started telling us about the four couples at a table nearby. All of them were drinking heavily. Margie and Boyd asked us to watch these people because within a half hour they would all throw their house keys into the center of the table. They then took napkins and blindfolded all the men. One by one each man would pick up a key off the table. Whatever woman's home the key belonged to, that man would go home with her that night. These couples did this every Friday night. Boyd and Margie said they had been asked to join this group but refrained from doing so, although they were tempted particularly when they had argument. Well, as we watched the keys all went into the middle of the table, blindfolds came on the men and keys were pulled. They called their club "The Exclusive Marin County Key Club"—not a very original name. We never went back to that club again for dinner because it was kind of repulsive. California definitely was more liberal than Minnesota in the early '50s.

(Boyd and Margie were awfully good to a couple of poor kids from God's Country!) One weekend they took us to a gigantic orange, lime, and lemon orchard belonging to a wealthy doctor friend of theirs. We picked oranges for the first time in our lives because there are no orange trees in Minnesota! The oranges tasted so different picked and eaten right off a tree. They were unbelievably good. (It is amazing what thrills a couple of nerds from Minnesota had.)

THE REHABILITATION CENTER S-1

REHABILITATION CENTER

Jane and Jenny, the two beautiful redhead twin sisters, did a fabulous job with all the patients. They taught many patients things like painting and molding clay. Most of these patients had never been exposed to outside interests of this kind. I saw patients who never played ping-pong before become unbelievable players. At that time I thought I was pretty good but there were two or three of them that would drub me every time. I saw aggressive patients calm down completely because of the patience the nurses and medics took explaining to these patients about the subject involved. They actually taught a new trade to some of the patients, such as carpentry. (How the instructors did it with all the sharp tools, I do not know—and none of the tools were ever stolen.) I remember patients with absolutely no confidence in themselves change completely, particularly after the "clique" left. Most of the patients were only at S-1 for a few months but what a change in making some of these patients into confident people again who took pride in themselves. The patients were hardly ever capable of being returned to combat duty but a few were able to return to active duty. Patients were mostly sent to state hospitals or released to relatives. Some were discharged into their own care which meant that they were released to society. Some of these releases were scary. There were instances of previous discharged patients robbing stores. I mentioned before that some began living on skid row and two committed suicide while I was at S-1.

One day a patient in the lower level tried to tear off Jane's clothes. He probably would have tried to rape her but two other patients stopped him. This one time there was no medical corpsman close by which was rare. But these two patients really did a job on this fellow. They punched him and held him to the floor until medics came with a straightjacket. No other patient ever tried again to touch one of the twins because they had their "patient" body guards with them at all times.

One other patient tried to climb the two-story-high mesh metal walls of the open basketball area. He was outside by himself shooting baskets. He stopped and started climbing. One of the nurses came out and saw him and then called my office. He had reached the top of the two-story mesh wall and was caught in the barbed wire on top. He started yelling and the MPs came. We had a fire engine come over and raise their moving stairs to the height of the barbed wire. This guy was so wrapped up in the wire it took a half hour to cut him free. He kept pleading that he would never do this again. He cried and said crying that he was sorry and asking us to help him. It was really quite laughable and pitiful at the same time. No one ever tried to climb out of S-1 this way ever again!

MENTAL STRESS ON MEDICS

Another close friend was David F. David was a draftee and arrived at S-1 about the same I did. Frosty was the nickname we gave him. He was a total extrovert—outgoing, humorous, and it was literally a laugh a minute when Frosty was around. He was from Iowa and we often reminisced about Minnesota versus Iowa football games. Bev and I had Frosty over to the apartment for dinner quite a few times. Bev absolutely adored him. He was a joy to be around. In the beginning Frosty seemed to relish being inside the ward and even more so after the "clique" was gone. The patients were responding to being treated as human beings and the ward was really running smoothly. I assigned Frosty to take patients to the main hospital for dental and medical appointments. The patients really responded to his direction and the orders that he gave them. We never got a call from any department in the main hospital about an S-1 patient acting up when Frosty was along with them—which was not true of other medics escorting patients to appointments at the main hospital. But about six months of Frosty being inside S-1, he changed. He suddenly became an introvert. He became short-tempered and hostile to patients and other medics. Everyone noticed this change. In private Captain Passage talked to him at great length quite a few times about this situation, but it did not help. Finally he slapped a patient who was acting up in the cafeteria. Later he apologized and said that he was sorry. Finally he was transferred to a medical ward in the main hospital with very light duty. Frosty never recovered from his time at S-1. He was transferred to Korea after one month. We had asked him to write to us once he got to Korea but he never did. We never heard from him again. This happened to quite a few medics after being in the closed environment continually for a few months.

UNUSUAL PATIENTS

One new patient, Elmo M., who had been on the ward less than one day, was discovered to have taken food, plastic utensils, cup, and plate from the cafeteria plus he took a stapler, note pad, business cards, a doctor's coat all from a new doctor's office (when he was being interviewed by this doctor). All of these stolen things were hidden in his maroon patient clothing. It seemed unbelievable that he could have carried this much stuff around undetected. After he left the doctor's office, Elmo walked down the first floor hall near the nurses' station. As he walked by, he dropped the stapler on the floor. He went back to pick it up and all hell broke loose and literally everything fell out of his pockets. He was really watched closely after that and never left alone. Upon reading his previous case history, Elmo had stolen lots of things from other soldiers in Korea. When he was shipped to Japan, it had not stopped. While being interviewed again by a doctor in Japan, he took the doctor's glasses, eraser, a pad and pen, and even a wristwatch lying on the doctor's desk (I guess the doctor was looking at his watch for a specific length of time for each patient). This young man was a true kleptomaniac. We tried ECT treatments and it did not help. One time in the ECT treatment room, he took a jar of Vaseline, some tongue compressors, and the wallet from one of the medics who was holding him down. After that Elmo was sent quickly to a state hospital.

VISITORS

The S-1 patients' visitors were interesting. Some were even sicker than the patients. There are a couple of sayings: "People who are similar have an affinity for each other," and another one, "Men and women who are married for a very long time begin to look alike and act alike." In the case of the visitors to S-1 both statements were true. Most of the S-1 visitors were wives of patients. We were not allowed to body search any visitor but we could ask questions. Questions like: Do you have anything in your purse or on your person to give to the patient? Many times they would stammer and tell us yes because the patient told them that he wanted a nail file and cigarettes the last time they were here, so they brought them. We would explain nicely that neither item was allowed for patients to have on a closed ward. Sometimes they would argue but usually they gave up the items. Of course, sometimes they lied and we would find the items later and take them from a patient. Bringing food or care packages were not allowed but many visitors brought these items anyway. One time in the visitors' room a couple tried to disrobe and have sex. We had to literally pull them apart. They could not understand why they could not make love in the visitors' room because it had been three weeks since they had a "roll in the sack"! They were allowed to kiss each other but that was it. A few visiting women waiting to see a patient would try to seduce the medic who was at the reception desk. Some came right out and said they were starved for sex or love and asked if the medic would help them out. One really ugly gal said to a medic that she did not have any panties on and would he like a peek!

Then she said that she had a car outside and they could do "it" in her car. She wanted to know what time he got off and she would wait for him. To my knowledge no one ever did—but who knows? Some of these gals were cute. A few visitors in general conversation said they were seeing a consultant or seeing a psychiatrist themselves. Others acted really strangely—talking to themselves and answering their own questions. Because we could not search a visitor, many did bring a knife or similar object and then gave it to the patient. But in most cases these items were found and taken away before harm was done.

TENNIS LESSONS

My tennis background: In high school my partner and I had won the City of Minneapolis Tennis Championship, then the Twin City Championship and then the regional. Finally we made it to the state finals being held at the University of Minnesota. We had already badly beaten our opponents in the finals three times earlier during the year. Plus we were undefeated for the year. So our chances looked mighty good to win the big one. We were scheduled to play our match at 11:00 a.m. on a Saturday morning. But by 11:00 my partner, Glenn, had not shown up for the match. The day before the big match, Glenn and I had talked about meeting at 10:00 a.m. for a warm up. I found a phone and tried Glenn's house but there was no answer. The tournament director waited until 11:30 a.m.—still no Glenn? We, of course, lost the state championship by default. Another thing that hurt a little was that besides beating this team three times previously and losing by default, they were from Bev's high school in Minneapolis, Southwest, and they had won the state championship the year before as juniors. I found out later that Glenn went to a Russian lecture of some sort at the University and he had forgotten completely our match. Glenn was a super brain and super athlete, but unfortunately his mind was sometimes up in a cloud, and it certainly was on that Saturday morning.

I went out for the Brooke Army Hospital's tennis team. I thought I was pretty good but learned I was lousy compared to all these southern boys who had much more experience having played tennis year round. We in Minnesota only had three to four months of practicing time. After one week on the Brooke's team, I got bumped off the team by a Junior Davis Cup winner. He was a young man from Florida and had played one year of tennis at U of Florida.

At Jane the rehab nurse's suggestion I started giving tennis lessons to patients twice a week. Jane had seen me playing tennis after work at the courts nearby one day. She thought the therapy for patients would be good. I taught men, up to three men at one time, two days a week and also taught two women and a nurse another day. After a few weeks some of the men became very good. In singles two patients became so good that they even beat me. I never was very good in singles—only doubles. We actually then had doubles tournaments with prizes. We had a list of patients a page long who wanted lessons. At the end of a month we had patients from S-1 playing the medical ward patients. Guess who won? The S-1 team of patients won! Maybe the medical patients feared what the S-1 patients might do if they lost? We had great equipment for the patients which was all supplied by the main hospital. The nurses were amazed at the change in the tennis patients' attitudes and the progress the patients made returning to being normal. Three patients recovered completely, two went back to duty, and one was discharged. Captain Passage called me into her office and said how great the results were from the patients playing tennis. She said that the officer staff had never thought of the idea before and the results were fantastic. Even Colonel Later who said very little ever to me or anyone else called me into his "inner sanctum" for a short talk. He said, "Pat, keep up those tennis lessons and maybe we will not have any more sick patients, just medical patients with tennis elbow!!" He then laughed. He did not laugh very often. I have to admit I was very happy and pleased with the success of the project. That night when I came home and told Bev, she said that I was walking two feet off the ground.

INCIDENTS AFTER THE "CLIQUE" ARE GONE

The "clique" was gone but we still had a few serious emergencies. One day in the rehab area a patient pulled out a knife. (We had no idea where he got it because he had not had any visitors.) He did stab another patient and then a medic. He cut them both not severely but they were both bleeding badly. Another medic tried to take the knife away and got stabbed in the leg. The emergency bell rang and I heard what was happening. We brought a mattress down to the lower level and found the patient was standing all by himself near a wall slashing at anyone who was within a six- to eight-foot radius. I took the twin-size mattress and with another medic's help we held the mattress in front of us and rushed the patient. He stabbed the mattress instead of one of us. We brought him to the floor with the air knocked out of him. He dropped the knife and we put him in a straightjacket, gave him a shot, and he was out. I still have his knife after all these years.

Another incident occurred in the dining room. A very sullen patient named Jimmie, who was only about five feet three inches tall and weighed about 125 pounds, for no reason went berserk. He screamed that his food was alive with bugs and snakes. He threw his plate against the wall, then picked up his chair and threw it against the wall. When the chair fell, it hit another patient who then started screaming and crying at the same time. Now we had two patients going wild. Just then a big medic tried to restrain the little guy. The little guy, Jimmie, picked up the 250-pound medic over his head and slammed him against the wall. I came running in to the dining room just as two other medics went after Jimmie. He swung one of them by grabbing his arms and heaving him over tables and people. The other medic tried to hold on to him. All I could see were four legs and I tackled them all. I got Jimmie down on his stomach and sat on him until we got him into a straightjacket.

There was another story about a patient becoming violent. A nurse on the first floor was giving a patient a shot and suddenly he hit her and threw her onto a couch nearby. Fortunately she was not hurt. Another nurse nearby rang the emergency bell and called my office. I came running down the hall as the wild man was screaming, "You shot me; you shot me. I'm going to die." He was jumping up and down and flailing his arms. This guy weighed about 200 pounds and was maybe five feet eight inches tall. Just then I yelled *stop* as loud as I could. He looked at me and started to charge. I dove at him low, he threw his arms up in the air, and I hit him with my right shoulder at his knees. He went down like a sack of potatoes. I flipped him over and got a half- nelson hold on him, pushing his face into the floor. Just then more medics came and we gave him a shot to knock him out. Then we put him in a straightjacket and into a seclusion room.

When a mental patient really goes berserk, their strength is super human. Like Superman they can literally leap over tall buildings, or they think they can. But their reflexes are very slow. Because I never got hurt during these scuffles with the patients and was able to subdue the patients, the nurses asked me why. After discussion it was determined that my training from wrestling in school enabled me to better understand "take down" and handling violent patients. They suggested that I should teach wresting techniques to the medics.

WRESTLING LESSONS

So once a week for two hours I showed the medics how to take down a berserk patient without either them or the patient getting hurt badly—if at all. We did this in the rehab area. We had the cushioned mats that were used for exercising patients placed on the floor. Naturally during these two-hour sessions, no patients were allowed in the rehab unit. Teaching the medics to take down a patient was not difficult. Most of the medics caught on quite easily. I created different situations that had happened in the past on the ward and how to handle each one. Some medics liked it so well they wanted to actually learn how to wrestle competitively. It was a fun time and really helped the medics and the patients. Prior to this, no training on handling of violent patients were ever discussed nor were solutions to the various problems. The best part was that no medics ever got seriously hurt after my training program.

Humorously when I started this program I told the medics what happened to me when I wrestled in high school. I was on the wrestling team for our high school and made it to the finals in the state wrestling championship. I was wrestling at the 145-pound level. I was leading my opponent in the third period of the match by 9 points to 0. While I was riding my opponent, he went off the mat. We were then back in the center of the mat in the main arena. There was only thirty seconds left in the match and I would win the match and the championship if nothing else happened— well, it did. I stupidly rode him from my left on his right side. I had never ridden anyone from the left in my three years of wrestling. I always rode from the right, which was the normal way to ride from the top position. The referee said, "Wrestle." Well, my opponent sat back and pinned me! Unbelievable but true! Sure took the wind out of my sails! Oh, well, that's life! I was never a cocky person, but I was at that time, and look at the results. Today in high school and college the wrestlers ride differently on top position—basically in the middle of the opponent's back as he is below on his haunches, on his hands and knees. Oh, the memories of the good and the bad.

HUMOROUS AND NOT SO HUMOROUS

Some humorous incidents occurred when an S-1 patient was taken to the dental lab. A medic, of course, always accompanied an S-1 patient and stayed with him/her at all times during their treatment. One time Horace S., a nice little guy, was brought to the dental lab. Immediately everyone saw the maroon outfit and knew he was from S-1. All the other patients around Horace became excited and wanted to leave immediately. Even some of the dentists and nurses left until Horace was finished with his exam. There had been incidents of S-1 patients becoming somewhat wild during their dental procedure, so everyone outside of S-1 personnel was frightened of maroon-uniformed patients from S-1. Horace would not have hurt anyone—it was probably the other way around. Back in the '50s mental illness was feared by most people. Few understood mental illness and thought all mental patients should be locked away and the key thrown away. Everyone thought the disease was incurable. All this was terrible but so true at that time in history. Horace's dental work went fine with no problems.

Another time a female mental patient, Betty N., an army WAC, was taken to the dental lab in her maroon dress. She was covered by a sheet or coverlet that dentists used to cover patients before the start of their procedures. A medic was standing next to her. Another women came and sat in the chair next to Betty. Now picture this, all the patients were lined up in a row with no dividers between patients. There were at least ten dental examining stations that were all wide open. Many of the other patients, nurses, and dentists had seen Betty come in with her maroon dress and a medic attending but they had not paid any attention to the other new patient because Betty's maroon dress was covered. This new patient was given Novocain within about ten minutes. The new patient next to Betty started screaming over and over with her mouth full of cotton balls, "Oh, my God, does this ever hurt! Help me. Stop!" Everyone thought it was Betty because the two women were next to each other and the medic was now sitting on a stool between the two women. All the room went crazy. The regular patients wanted to get up and leave. Some of the patients actually did get up from their dental chairs and try to leave the area. Dentists and nurses all started to leave the area and even leave their patients. It was really crazy and laughable! Only a few patients and their dentists besides Betty's dentist and nurse stayed. Someone had called the MPs to come and said that an S-1 patient was crazy in the dental lab. The MPs arrived and someone pointed out the patient next to Betty was the one who was screaming and said she was an S-1 patient. The MPs started to remove her and found that she was not an S-1 patient. The woman had her mouth full of cotton balls and could hardly talk. Finally Betty's dentist said that this was not an emergency and Betty who was from S-1 was perfectly fine. The MPs still were not sure but did ask the other woman patient to please leave. The woman was the wife of a regular army sergeant who was in charge of cleaning the hospital. She was now outraged at her treatment. Betty did finally get her cavity fixed and quietly came back to wonderful S-1, totally unharmed by the sergeant's hysterical wife. Unfortunately, practically everyone outside of S-1 was fearful of the S-1 mental patients.

MORE HUMOR

The humor that some of the patients created was really many times fantastically funny. One patient, Bruce I., thought I was his father. He told everyone that I was his father and all the great times we had had fishing together and all the fish we caught. He said I was the greatest fisherman and had won a contest catching the biggest fish in Colorado, Bruce's home state. He told all that it was a forty-foot shark, the largest ever caught in Colorado. First of all, of course, there are no sharks in Colorado unless someone has a mounted trophy from California or someplace that sharks live. Secondly, I am the worst fisherman in the world. Fish do not like me! I have been fishing many times in the greatest fishing holes in God's Country, Minnesota—the land of 10,000 lakes and one hundred fish and I have caught nothing! Bev and I used to go fishing in one of the lakes near Minneapolis and she would catch fish after fish and I had nary a bite on my line. We would switch lines or poles or rods or whatever and still not a bite. When people hear this, they all want to take me fishing to a secluded, secret spot where there are millions of walleye pike (the best-tasting fish in the world but has lots of bones). Once we went to this fabulous spot and you can guess the rest. Everyone caught oodles and oodles of fish and I did not even get a nibble. Then there were a few times when people took me fishing and then they never caught any fish either. So I then became a jinx and they never wanted me to go fishing with them again. I am just a little paranoid myself! Back to Bruce and the outcome of his story. Well, he also selected a black nurse as his mother and my wife. He kept talking about his mom and dad and how great we were. By the way at that time I was twenty-three and the nurse was about twenty-five, and Bruce was regular army lieutenant, about thirty-five. These parental comments kept up until Bruce was sent home to Colorado to a state hospital near his real, good ol' mom and dad.

Another patient actually thought he was an army general. His name was—guess what—Doug MacArty. He even called himself General Mac. (His name was pretty close to a certain general at the same time who was not too popular with our President Harry S. Truman. These two, the president and General MacArthur, did not agree on how to handle the Korean War. Guess whose plan eventually won? Our esteemed president's.) Back to our General Mac. He went around ordering and dictating to everyone. We were all told to salute him and all superior officers at all times and to stand up straight and look like soldiers. Amazingly some patients actually went around saluting him, saying, "Yes, sir. No, sir!" The most interesting thing was a story that he told shortly before he left S-1. General Mac said that he had a top secret war plan and he would only confide this plan to a select few of us whom he trusted. His secret war plan was to conquer the enemy and capture all of North Korea. He said his plan was very complicated but could be accomplished overnight if his directions were followed. His plans included air strikes on specific targets and mass invasions in certain locations in North Korea. Possibly he was a genius and maybe his plan would have worked. We even started to believe him. He had been on General MacArthur's staff at one time as a chauffeur or a driver of some sort. He may have overheard some very important secrets. We will never know. He was transferred out in a strange way one night to an unknown destination. We all missed him a lot. He was fun and very interesting.

THE 300-POUND CANARY

We had a patient named Herbert who weighed over 300 pounds and was only about five feet five inches tall. He reminded me of the story of Humpty Dumpty because he looked like what I imagined Humpty Dumpty would look like. Herbert wanted to have the barbers bleach his hair. Naturally they would not. He would not tell why he wanted that bleach job. At meals he would gorge himself eating at the cafeteria. He ate as much as six other patients. Then after he had finished eating, he would skip and jump, huffing and puffing, around the first floor hall. He would dance around saying, "I am a pretty canary. I am a pretty canary. See me fly!" and he would wave his arms up and down as if trying to fly. We now figured out the reason why he wanted his hair bleached—he was to look like a canary! When he was told by a nurse or medic to stop these antics because he was bothering other patients, he then would say that we were all mean cats. He would repeat this over and over and over. One day he wanted a seventh plate of food and was told absolutely no by one of the cooks. So he went crazy screaming as loud as he could, "I hate you, I hate you, all you *bad cats*!" Then he said very quietly, "I am a 300-pound canary and I eat cats!" Then the funniest of all was when he said in a deep, deep voice, "Here kitty, kitty. Here kitty, kitty. Here kitty, kitty." He must have heard that old joke someplace and started to live the story. It was funny but he was serious! Herbert was with us a few more days and then was sent to a state hospital. We sent so many patients to state hospitals. I often wondered what their care was like and what happened to many of them.

PRISONER SECTION — INCIDENT
OUTSIDE S-1

Al R. was a soldier who was shot in the head in Korea while on patrol. He was treated at an emergency medical aid station in Korea. Then he was flown to Japan for surgery. He had to have radical surgery to remove the bullet located very near his brain. The surgery was successful but afterward he had a total personality change. Before his surgery he had been a jovial, happy, outgoing twenty-seven-year-old sergeant who planned to make a career in the army. After his operation in Japan he became sullen, withdrawn, actually mean and vicious. One day he took a swing and hit a corpsman who was trying to help him get into a wheelchair. Al was now somewhat bedridden but he was allowed to sit on the side of his bed, stand up, and walk a few steps or sit in a wheelchair. His doctor knew something was radically wrong with him but there was not a psychiatrist at this hospital to observe and recommend treatment. The plan was to send him to another hospital in Japan that had a psychiatrist who could help him. One day before he was to be transferred, the patient next to Al who was also badly wounded was moaning and asking for the nurse. Al said nothing, got out of bed, picked up a bed pan on the table nearby, and started hitting the other patient repeatedly in the head. The other patients in the ward said he hit the moaning patient at least thirty times. It took three corpsmen to restrain Al. He was given a sedative to knock him out. The other badly wounded patient died. Al was then flown in restraints to S-1 and put in the prisoner section. Colonel Later made the decision immediately for Al to have a series of ECT treatments. After the treatments Al seemed to be recovering very well. He became pleasant and cooperative. Well, during the week of his ECT treatments, Al had a very bad toothache and had to be sent to dental lab. He was handcuffed and accompanied by two MPs and one medic to the lab. The lab had a few private dental patient rooms and Al was brought to one of these. While examining Al, the dentist found he had a terrible abscessed tooth and it had to be treated before it could be repaired or removed. During the treatment when the dentist injected Novocain, Al tried to jump out of the chair and went crazy. He still had the handcuffs on and put his arms with the handcuffs over the dentist's head to choke him. The MPs and medic were there and stopped Al. That was the end of his treatment that day. The dentist said Al would have to be sedated before bringing him back to the lab or he would not ever treat him again. On the way back to S-1, Al tried to pull the gun out of the holster of one of the MPs and the gun went off. Fortunately, no one was shot. The next day Al was taken back to the dental lab, sedated, his tooth fixed, and returned back to S-1. Al completed his ECT treatments in the next week. He was very calm and seemed harmless but I will never know because a few days later while I was on my day off, Al was transferred out of S-1 to points unknown. We all wondered how the army was handling Al's murder of the patient in Japan. Was he ever prosecuted, or was the world told the patient died from a battle wound, or what?

INCIDENT AT OPEN WARD

Phil O. was a patient who had been at S-1 for a very short time suffering from amnesia, depression, and was recovering from a Korean War wound. Phil's right ear had been shot off and some damage was sustained on the right side of his face. It was decided by his doctor at S-1 that his condition was improving and medication was all he needed. So he was transferred to the open ward and then to be either back to duty or discharged in the near future. On the open ward patients are allowed weekend passes. On one of these passes Phil went into San Francisco with two other patients from the ward. While there he left his two friends and took off by himself to a bar in Chinatown. He got into a fight with a sailor also on leave. The police came and Phil ended up in jail. Phil was beaten pretty badly either at the bar or by the police and did not know his name or where he lived. He was not in uniform and had no identification on him. At S-1 Phil was first listed as AWOL from the open ward. Then a week later, he was discovered in jail. He did have his dog tags on but at first the police had paid no attention to them. While examining his wounds, they finally noticed the dog tags and figured out that he was a serviceman. They called MPs who checked with various bases around

SF and discovered who he was. Phil was then returned to S-1. His new doctor (the previous doctor was gone) recommended ECT treatments. The treatments worked great. Some family members came and he was discharged from the army.

INCIDENTS AT THE NEW S-1

One day when I was sitting in my office planning the schedule for the following week, I got a call from the nursing station on second floor that a patient was having a heart attack and he needed to be rushed to cardiology at once. So first I called cardiology telling them that we had an S-1 patient coming to them who had had a heart attack and for them to be prepared to help him. I then had two medics take the patient, Jerry, on a gurney to cardiology through the halls of the main Letterman Hospital. This transport was faster than having an ambulance come and take Jerry to cardiology. Jerry had been in army intelligence in Japan and overnight became delusional. He was first hospitalized in Japan and they were concerned about security at the hospital there and sent him on to S-1. His case was being handled exclusively by Colonel Later. He had been treated with deep insulin therapy and seemed to be doing okay. He was kept in a private room on the second floor away from everyone else. He had no history of a heart condition and seemed to be in perfect health. It was found at cardiology that he had all kinds of arterial blockages and would have to have a triple bypass to hopefully solve his heart problem. Jerry was kept in cardiology and was doing fine. Because of Jerry's background he had to have an MP assigned to his room at all times. About the third night after his surgery, the MP went down the hall to the men's room thinking Jerry was sleeping. When he came back, Jerry was gone. The MP reported that an S-1 patient had escaped from cardiology and he was dangerous! The whole hospital went nuts! Four hours later Jerry was found in the cardiology coffee break room smoking, drinking coffee, and seemed perfectly normal. No one had any idea where Jerry got the cigarettes and how he was able to get up out of bed and walk to the break room. He was transferred back to S-1 immediately. And believe it or not, about two weeks later Jerry was sent back to active duty.

We had another very interesting patient named Lee M. Lee had an invisible friend, Barney, who was with him all the time. They always ate together at every meal. Lee would always get two plates of food, one for himself and one for Barney. Barney had his favorite foods and Lee would get a double portion for Barney. Barney particularly liked fried chicken. Interestingly Lee was not fond of fried chicken because Lee thought fried foods were not good for you. If there was ice cream served, Lee would get a double portion for Barney because he loved ice cream. We would ask questions to Lee like, "What does Barney look like?" Lee's answer was, "You can see him. He is sitting right next to me!" We would ask him what clothes Barney had on today. Lee would say that they were just like his, maroon pants and maroon Ike jacket. This situation was much like Jimmy Stewart in the movie "Harvey," except Harvey was a six-foot-tall rabbit. Barney and Lee would play cards together all the time. Occasionally, Lee would get mad and say that Barney was cheating! This happened when they played blackjack more than any other card game. They talked together constantly about everything from politics to sports. Finally one day one of the nurses told Lee that he and Barney needed to take a shower together and put on a clean set of maroons. Lee answered, "I do not take a shower with anyone else, and who in the hell is Barney?" Lee was not nearly as much fun after that. We all missed Barney. Lee was sent to the open ward soon after that without Barney.

ANOTHER BIG REHAB AT S-1

Henry was one of the draftees assigned to S-1. Henry had been in premed at the University of Texas. He also played basketball his freshman year at Texas. In high school he made the second team all-state in basketball. Henry, we called him Tex, was about six feet five inches tall. So he was a really big guy back in the 1950s. Well, at that time I was teaching tennis to patients so I thought why not let Tex teach them basketball. Captain Passage and the twins thought it was a fabulous idea. So Tex started teaching three days a week for two hours in the afternoon. The patients loved it. Tex formed two teams with ten patients on each team. They were really getting pretty good and a couple of the patients who were going to be discharged did not want to leave because they were having so much fun. There were a few conflicts with patients but nothing serious. Tex was quite emphatic that if anyone became violent or started fights or became hysterical while playing they were off the teams for good. No one ever did and there were no problems. The patients wanted to play some other teams on the base at the Presidio. We tried to make some arrangements for games but it was squashed by the top brass at the hospital. They were afraid of repercussions. But the patients were allowed to play a team made up of S-1 medics a few times and the patients won every game. Things were getting better and better at the new psychiatric medical ward called S-1! (No one ever better call it an asylum for the insane again!) The patients were all ill with a disease that was treatable—just like the rest of the patients at Letterman Hospital.

BACK TO THE PRISONER SECTION

In the 1950s the lowest form and the worst kind of prisoner at S-1 was not a murderer but a dope addict! Even all the prisoners felt the same way and looked down on this type of prisoner. But these addicts were few and far between. We had one miserable guy named Alfonse R. (Maybe if my name was Alfonse, I would be miserable too.) His history was that he stole drugs, beat up the drugstore owner, and was caught. It had been Alfonse's first arrest. In court the judge gave him a choice of five years in jail or he could enlist in the army and the army would straighten him out. (The judge must have been an ex-army officer.) Naturally Alfonse took the Army route. After basic training he was sent to Korea. He then asked to be assigned to the medics although he had no medical background. They took him because more and more medics along with officers were being killed in Korea. Well, you can guess what happened next. He stole medical drugs and got caught again. When he got caught, he went totally off the wall, hallucinating, raving like a fool, seeing all kinds of snakes and monsters, and constantly screaming. He had to be placed in a straight-jacket most of the time. The doctors had no idea what drugs he had taken that would cause this type of crazy reaction. He was first sent to the medical station in Tokyo for observation and then sent to S-1. At that time drug addicts were very rare so there was no proper treatment process for this kind of illness. Alfonse was finally acting normal at S-1. I did not know the treatment the colonel recommended but it seemed to work. Then one day the nurses were in the prisoner section giving patients different medication. The cart with the drugs and other medical equipment was outside Alfonse's cell. He reached through the door bars when a nurse was not looking and stole some drugs. One of the medic corpsmen saw him take the drugs. So his cell was opened to take the drugs away. He then swallowed a whole bunch of pills before they could take them all away. Humorously, some of the pills he grabbed and swallowed were for constipation. Boy, did they work on Alphonse. He never left the toilet for a whole day. Shortly, after that he was picked up from the S-1 prisoner section by MPs and sent to an army prison.

ANOTHER UNIQUE PATIENT

Joseph L. was a "fly boy" who came to S-1 from an air force basic training base in California. He had a nervous breakdown during his eighth week of training. This happened when he was on an obstacle course and fell on his head and was knocked out. When Joseph came in the base hospital, he was delusional. He did not know his name or where he was. After a while he remembered his name was Joseph and said he was from California—which was true. But he was very depressed. Joseph had spells of constantly crying. He kept talking about all kinds of crazy things like seeing monsters, giant snakes, and he began shaking all the time. He was then sent to us for treatment. Joseph was put on a series of ECT treatments. After about four treatments he started talking Italian! Then he never spoke English and did not understand English. He gestured with his hands like some old Italian person would do. Fortunately, one of the nurses spoke fluent Italian and was able to communicate with him. He knew his name was Joseph but thought he was lost in Italy and could not find his way home. When he went to the cafeteria to eat, he could not understand why there was no Italian food or no wine with every meal. When the Italian-speaking nurse was not around, it was really funny trying to communicate with Joseph. It was interesting for a few days trying to communicate with him. After two more treatments though, Joseph was finally himself and remembered everything that had happened. But he still remained frightened of many things—but no more snakes, monsters, and he never spoke Italian again. We asked him if he spoke Italian and he answered that he spoke just a few words that he had picked up from his parents. His parents lived near San Diego and came to San Francisco to bring Joseph home. He was released to their care. This was the only case I remember of a patient speaking a foreign language and thinking they were in another country.

ONE MORE FLY BOY OR FLY GIRL STORY

Air force sergeant Cliff H. was sent to S-1 under a rather strange set of circumstances. Cliff had been a training

non-com at a local air force base. He had been in the
air force with a distinguished record before WWII. One
evening an officer popped into Cliff's private room in his
barracks at the base and found Cliff was dressed up like a
woman! He first laughed at Cliff and then asked if he was
going to a costume party because it was near Halloween.
Cliff stammered, bowed his head, and said yes. The officer
asked where the party was because it sounded like fun.
Cliff stammered again and then started to whimper and
sob. Now Cliff was a very big guy, maybe 260 pounds and
six feet two, so the situation was really very bizarre. This
great big guy dressed as a woman with lots of makeup,
crying, sobbing on and on. The officer told Cliff to sit
down and talk to him. At first Cliff refused but then did
as the officer requested. The officer asked how long this
behavior had been going on and Cliff answered that it
had been for most of his life—he had wanted to be a girl.
He told the officer that he had only been cross-dressing
in the air force for about four years but no one knew it.
Cliff told him that he would sneak out very late at night
and come back very early before anyone saw him. Cliff
said that since he was a small child he had liked girls'
clothes. He said that for all of his life he had tried fighting this desire to be a woman. The officer told Cliff that
he needed help now and that this behavior would not be
tolerated by the air force. Cliff reluctantly agreed to seek
help. He saw a doctor at the base and then was sent to
S-1. Now at S-1 he had treatments but afterward he told
the doctors that he still wanted to be a girl. He tried a
few times to sneak into the women's section to try to get
one of their dresses. He used to hang out by the women's
section a lot. One day a cart of clean clothes was being

brought into the women's section and he stole one dress from the cart. Cliff took it into an empty room and put it on. He then started walking around the halls totally elated. Of course Cliff was stopped immediately by the nurses and medics. It was quite a sight to see. Here was this great big guy in a dress that was way too small for him floating around the halls at S-1. Cliff had even more treatments but nothing helped. Finally he was discharged from S-1 on his own. A few months later he (or she) stopped back at S-1. He was stylishly dressed with lots of makeup and happy as could be. He told us that he (or she) was now working in a department store in women's cosmetics. In San Francisco, anything was possible for anyone to be whoever they wished to be. It was a wide open city!

ANOTHER VERY PATHETIC STORY ABOUT A SOLDIER FIGHTING NEAR THE 34TH PARALLEL IN KOREA

The medical file on Corporal Hugh M. supplied the following information: Hugh M. was being sent to S-1 as a catatonic patient. He was a corporal in the infantry. He joined the army in 1949 at the age of twenty-two and had been in Korea for over five months—all the time on patrol or fighting skirmishes. His company had been pinned down with heavy artillery for over three days with no rest, limited food, and no warm clothes in the worst winter in Korea. He ran out of ammunition and none of his buddies around him would give him any of the limited ammo they had left. His fellow soldiers said Hugh was kind of a weird guy and had kept shooting at nothing until he finally ran out of ammo. They did not want to spare their ammo with this character who was wasting all his bullets. Hugh finally started yelling, "I will kill you. I will kill you," over and over, again and again. He then got out of his trench, pointed his gun straight ahead, and started saying loudly, "Bang, bang, pow, pow, bang, bang, pow, pow." Then he ran forward about twenty feet, stopped, and again yelled, "Bang, bang, pow, pow." He did this repeatedly for another twenty yards. He must have really thought he was shooting and maybe hitting the enemy. His buddies kept yelling to stop but he paid no attention to them.

Believe it or not, but his buddies said the Chinese who were about forty yards in front of Hugh got up, looked at this crazy guy, and then started to retreat. They did not shoot back, just kept looking back at him. They must have thought he was really a crazy, wild man! The Chinese were yelling something at him but his buddies said they had no idea what was being said because it was in Chinese. His buddies, seeing what happened, finally ran after him and were able to subdued Hugh before some Chinese soldier changed his mind and shot Hugh. Hugh was then sent to Japan to recover. The doctors tried to figure out what happened to him because the whole situation was really weird. But in the Japanese hospital he would not talk. He just sat staring ahead all the time and had to be fed, etc. After two weeks in Japan. He was sent to us. He was given a series of ECTs and it helped. He became a quiet, gentle soul. He ate all his meals with no help and followed whatever he was told to do. Hugh did not remember anything about his time in Korea. Hugh was finally released to the care of his parents.

MORE LIFE OUTSIDE OF S-1

MAXI THE JEWISH KITTY

We wanted a pet. Both Bev and I had been raised with pets. Bev always had cats and I always had a dog. The owner of a Jewish deli near our apartment, Max, had a litter of kittens. The kittens were all short-haired, black, with white chests. He took them to a vet for only one reason—he wanted only a male cat and no more females to have more kittens. But he could not tell the sex of the kittens so he took them to the vet for identification. Well, the vet said they were all females except for one male, so Max kept that one. So we took one of the females and called her Maxi after the owner of the Deli. Maxi the kitten was absolutely adorable and the smartest animal I had ever seen. We had a sandbox for Maxi as a kitten. But as Maxi grew older, she became an outside cat and stayed in only at night. Maxi slept with us on our twin bed every night. It was really just a little crowded. Maxi was really growing and we took her to the vet for shots because she was an outside cat. Guess what? Maxi was a boy! Were we ever surprised and so was the deli owner. He wanted our male cat back. But we, of course, said no. He even offered us free food of our choice for a week. We still said no. (Coincidentally, the kitten he kept was a female and he had already given it away. So he still wanted a male cat. Our guess was he wanted to keep out mice and rats from his store!) About three months later Maxi disappeared. We looked all over for him. He would normally come like a dog when we called him for dinner or whatever. But no Maxi came. So we went to the animal rescue a few days later and there was Maxi! He was in the back of a cage cowering and shivering. We asked the rescue people where he was found. The shelter people said that he was discovered in Golden Gate Park. (If you remember, the park was a less than a block from our apartment.) He had been "treed" by a pack of six or more barking dogs. Someone running in the park saw Maxi in a tree and the dogs barking and called the animal rescue. They came and brought him down. The rescuers estimated that he had been up the tree at least three days. We took poor Maxi home but his mind was totally gone because of fear—just like some of the S-1 patients back from Korea. We tried keeping him inside for two more weeks but there was no change. He had to be hand fed. When he used the sand-box, he put his two front feet in the box and the rest of his body outside the sandbox on the tile floor and relieved himself. Finally we had to send him to "kitty heaven." I have since painted a picture of Maxi using a picture I had of him sitting on a stool in the garden of our old apartment house. He was a beautiful, special, Jewish deli kitty.

FINAL DAYS AT S-1
THE REHAB CENTER

ABOUT HUAN

Huan, who was one of the civilian nurse's assistants on the ward, and I became the best of friends. I discussed a little about Huan earlier in the book. He wanted to be doctor or have his own restaurant. Huan also backed me with the "clique." Huan was a Chinese American born in the USA and very proud of it. Huan invited Bev and I plus some other draftees whom he liked to his home for dinner. He constantly would try out new dishes on us, some Chinese and some American Chinese. Most were delicious. Some such as turtle soup and frog legs were different but really tasty. It was the first time two kids from Minnesota had ever eaten these delicacies. I would guess that at the time Huan was about forty-five years old. (With the Chinese age is hard to tell because they all look so young.) He was not married but had been dating the same little Chinese girl, Mia Ling, for ten years. She was a secretary at the Chinese embassy. She would also be at his house for dinner with us many times. They had plans to open a restaurant together. Huan would be the chef and Mia Ling the hostess. They were saving their money to open the restaurant by 1954. That was their goal.

On the ward Huan would just touch a disturbed patient and they would calm down immediately. God definitely blessed Huan with a gift of helping disturbed people. Huan was also a church- going Christian. I remember when I interceded with some of "clique" hurting patients, he would say afterward that he would have liked to have helped but he had no position or authority. The civilian employees who helped were treated like second-class citizens most of the time. They were given many of the dirty jobs of cleaning floors, restrooms, and messes that patients made. They were not treated as equals by most of the army staff. I said before that the civilian employees were black, Hispanic, or Oriental. Huan was so humble and appreciative of anything kind said to him or done for him. I have never before or since S-1 met a person who actually glowed like Huan Young. He and Mia Ling did open their restaurant in Chinatown in 1954 as planned. I was never there but Huan wrote Bev and I that it was a great success. He also wrote how much he missed us and hoped to see us again in this world, but if not, certainly in heaven. God bless you, Huan Young.

BORIS THE PARTY KING

One of the real characters that I met at Letterman was Boris. Boris was born in Poland. He came to America as a small boy with his family just before WWII. This was the time when Hitler was marching through Poland. He and his family all escaped. His father had been a shoemaker and had saved just enough money to bring his family to

America. They had relatives in New York and who helped them get started with a new life in the USA. In 1948 Boris joined the Army after high school. He became a medic and was assigned to surgery at Letterman. He was now a corporal and surgical assistant and loved it. His long-range plans after the army were to go into medicine if he had the money. Bev and I met him through a friend, Mike, one of the draftees at S-1. Both Boris and Mike were Polish and went to the same high school and attended the same Catholic church in New York City. They both had real Brooklyn accents, with all the "dats" and "dues" and "ain'ts." He was a great fun guy who really enjoyed life and was having a ball at Letterman. Boris was also a good singles tennis player. He and I played tennis quite a bit. He even helped me with training the S-1 patients. Boris had the idea of forming a Letterman tennis team and we would play other army bases nearby. So we did. Boris was the captain and he arranged all the matches. Boris and I played doubles together and also singles. As a team we were not very good. We won a few matches but were beaten more often than we won. It was still a lot of fun and lots of laughs. One of the problems with Boris was that he would start laughing while telling some wild story and we would all start laughing and forget about playing tennis. Boris loved to party for any reason. Sometimes during our tennis matches he would make a batch of Moscow mules, the hottest drink in California during the war. It was vodka and ginger beer. The drink was supposed to be a shot of vodka and the balance ice and ginger beer in a six-ounce glass. Boris reversed the mix all the time. Then he put the drinks in a thermo container with ice and brought them to the tennis matches.

We would drink this instead of water. It went down like water and looked like water, sort of! No wonder we lost so many matches. About every three months Boris would have a lamb roast like they did in the "old country". We would all chip in to buy a whole lamb, potatoes, onions, celery and carrots to put inside the lamb. Then the lamb was put on a spit. We had to have Moscow mules for refreshments while the lamb was cooking. Bev and I always went to the lamb roasts along with our friends. We were the only married couple invited. The twins from rehab and some other cute nurses from S-1 and surgery usually came too. We always had at least fifteen to twenty people at the lamb roasts. Mike always played a fiddle and Boris would dance Polish polkas. He would teach us all the dances and we would sing Polish songs that he taught us. We in turn taught Boris the Pennsylvania polka. These were experiences I will never forget. I still remember a few Polish words that Boris and Mike taught me. But most of these words were a little "off color." Boris and one of the twins, Jane, had a "thing going." He could charm any gal. As I said before, officers and non-coms are not supposed to mix—that is the reason that the lamb roasts were never at the Presidio or was anyone ever in uniform. I hope Boris and Jane did marry after their time in service and then had little Borises.

S-1 PATIENTS' PICNICS

The twins from rehab came up with the idea of patient picnics to help remind them of home. These were held on weekends. Food was prepared by the cooks in the kitchen at S-1. Only patients, both male and female, who were getting close to being discharged or going back to active duty or discharged to family members, were allowed to attend. Of course medics, nurses, sometimes civilian personnel and once a doctor even tagged along. In some cases, if a patient's spouse or relative was living locally, they were invited. Everyone had a good time and always wanted to come every time we were having another picnic. It seemed that many of the patients who attended actually recovered even quicker. It was amazing. We never had one problem or an incident with any patient at these affairs. All the picnics were held on the vast grounds of the Presidio, most walking distance from S-1. We sang songs and had a few simple games that they played along with the picnics. It was a little like school that if the patients were good they were allowed these privileges. The patients seemed to get better and better. It was becoming more and more like a true rehabilitation center. It was certainly not an asylum like it was when I first came to S-1.

CAPTAIN PASSAGE/CORPORAL SVEN

Corporal Sven had been Captain Passage's secretary for about three months before I arrived at S-1. It was not common knowledge to most people at S-1 that the Captain and Corporal had more than a working relationship. First, if it was discovered, they would both be chastised and possibly demoted. Certainly one or the other, probably Sven, would have been shipped to another base. Sven confided to me that he and the captain were having an outside relationship. Sven was about ten years younger than the captain and they really did care for each other. But at S-1 they were all business at all times. Sven had joined the army in

January 1950, so his three-year hitch was over at the same time my two-year period was up. Being from Minnesota, Sven and I had a lot in common, especially Minnesota football. Sven had tried out for football at Minnesota as a halfback when he was a freshman but was not big enough or fast enough. I envied him for even trying out. He had been a really good halfback in high school in Mankato, Minnesota. I used to practice wrestling on Saturdays with the University of Minnesota wrestling team when I was in high school and knew that to play football you had to have size and lots of speed. I had neither. Some of the wrestlers in the heavier weights also played football and I learned a lot from them. I will tell more about Sven and the captain a little later. Captain and Sven both wanted to join Boris's parties but were afraid of being caught. (It would have been an impossible situation because the captain was in charge of everyone at S-1.)

TOP SECRET NEW PATIENT AT S-1

In the fall of 1952 we had the wildest situation happen. We discovered that all the civilian employees with anything unusual in their past history were being investigated. At the end of the investigation any civilian employees with as little as a traffic ticket were discharged. We lost about half the civilians on the ward including two stenographers in the adjoining office. Fortunately my friend Huan was okay. But this new rule really caused problems because this all happened unexpectedly and we now were terribly shorthanded and we were now down about fifteen civilian employees. Then late one night a few days later a new patient was secretly brought into our ward.

He had been heavily guarded by plain-clothes men all in dark suits and all with guns. There were also six MPs around him at all times. He was in a straightjacket, hallucinating, and talking incoherently. His records said his name was John Doe (really imaginative!), forty-two years old, no rank or with any other information given. The records said that he needed mental assistance. Everyone remaining on the ward, both army and civilian personnel, had to sign a secret agreement that anything we heard would not be repeated. We could talk to each other but not to anyone outside of S-1. John Doe was on our ward less than three weeks and Colonel Later saw him exclusively. Doe did have deep insulin therapy. At the beginning he was very hysterical, jabbering constantly, saying numbers and deadlines that must be met. None of it made much sense. The men in black never left his side. John Doe was kept in a second floor room by himself with no contact with other patients. After completing his series of treatments, John Doe was shipped out to places unknown—this was all done late at night. Weeks later we heard through the grapevine that he was an atomic bomb scientist from New Mexico. The men in black were secret service agents. This was later confirmed by Red, Colonel Later's secretary, but we were to say nothing to anyone. We all thought that the government was afraid of what John Doe might say about the bomb and how it was developed. This might have been the main reason but there may have been another something else. I later heard that the American public was never completely told about the terrible effects of the radiation from the bombs that were dropped on Hiroshima and Nagasaki, Japan. The hundreds of thousand of Japanese people who died or suffered horrible effects from the radiation were never completely explained to the American public. The government acted like they were surprised and had little knowledge of these radiation effects but they all knew from the experiments on animals what would probably happen. There was no cure or real help for these devastated people. Prior to the bombs being dropped by our B29 planes, experiments were being performed on many dogs in a secret location in Nevada. The poor dogs literally went through hell for many months before the date to drop the bomb. So our government did have a good idea how bad the effect of bomb radiation would be. There have since been books and documentary TV programs about this subject. The one great thing was it did end the war overnight with Japan and helped end the entire WWII much more quickly. Maybe, as terrible as the situation was, it was worth shocking the Japanese government into surrendering. The Japanese had said they would never surrender under any condition. The atomic bomb made the conditions totally impossible for the Japanese to retaliate! The Japanese military were absolutely ruthless, horrible people with no ethics or humility toward others. The bomb solved an impossible situation for the United States and our Allies.

ONE MORE UNIQUE INCIDENT

On a rare occasion two women patients in the women's section would get into a fight. There was this one big gal, a sergeant and a career WAC, who must have been a borderline lesbian. She tried to get romantically involved with a cute, petite WAC who was placed in S-1 because she had had a nervous breakdown in basic training. This big sergeant tried to fondle and caress the breast of the young, smaller WAC. The little WAC said, "No, do not touch me." The sergeant would not stop. So the little gal hauled off and hit the big woman smack in the nose. The big gal screamed, "She hit me! She hit me." Blood was running all over her and the floor. But fortunately a nurse saw the whole thing. She tried to stop the fight but the little gal kept hitting the big gal. Finally medics came and broke up the fight. The WAC sergeant was put in a seclusion room. A few days later she was transferred to a state hospital. After about one month the tough little WAC recovered completely and was assigned back to duty.

CHRISTMAS AT S-1

When you are in the service being away from home at Christmas is, without questions, the toughest time of the year. Christmas was for many of the patients very difficult as well. We had a tree in the lobby but no trees were allowed inside the ward proper. We did try to have a happy atmosphere at all times. Patients were not allowed to have gifts but we did have great food, cookies, cakes, and all the goodies. We sang Christmas carols quite a few times just before Christmas. One of the patients wanted to be Santa Claus and took a pillowcase and filled it with all kinds of funny stuff that was allowed on the ward. Then Santa asked if anyone wanted to sit on his knee and talk to him. Believe it or not, a few patients actually came up and talked to him. Christmas dinner was special with every kind of food anyone could imagine. The cooks had asked the patients if there was anything special they had at home and would like and many responded. The cooks came up with an unbelievable menu for all nationalities, both in main courses and desserts. Considering the place we were all in for the holiday, it was a pretty darn good Christmas for everyone.

Bev and I had our first Christmas tree. It was a white little flocked tree. We put lights and some homemade ornaments on the tree. We bought each other a few inexpensive gifts. It was great! We went to Dick and Bugs for Christmas dinner.

GOING-AWAY PARTY

Captain Passage threw a party for Sven, her secretary, just before he and I were discharged. The party was a *thank you* for all the things we had both done for her and the whole S-1 unit. She also invited Master Sergeant Mathew M. and his wife. The party was at a cliff-side restaurant south of San Francisco. We first met at the mountaintop location for cocktails and hors d'oeuvres. The idea was for us all to see our last sunset together in California before we left for home. Captain Passage was definitely a romantic. There were lots of hugs and kisses and booze. We then left for the restaurant. The food was superb plus they had a dance band. We then danced and drank until about 2:30 a.m. Sergeant M.'s wife, Barbara, was the quietest person I ever met—until she got loaded! Then she had a total personality change and became a total extrovert. She danced wildly by herself and/or anyone in the place. She then kept propositioning every man she danced with and there were many. Her husband just sat and drank paying absolutely no attention to her. As I said, the party ended about 2:30 a.m. Captain Passage said how much she appreciated all I had done to change S-1 into a true rehabilitation center for disturbed patients and turning it into nearly a country club. She said she would love and remember me always as one of her best friends in her life. She then said that tomorrow (this was my last week) she wanted to talk to me before I go.

The next day she called me into her office and said that if I would reenlist in the army and stay at S-1 within three months she would get me an emergency battlefield commission as a second lieutenant or a least a warrant officer. She said that S-1 had a very unique classification, very much like a battlefield command, and a commission was possible. She had previously clarified this with Colonel Later and he agreed 100 percent and wanted me to know this. I have to admit I was really very tempted. Every young man would like to be an officer. It is something you dream about. Bev and I talked about it but we both were anxious to see everyone at home and start our life together back in Minnesota. So at the end of the week we headed home. I left with many fond memories of the people at Letterman and particularly at S-1, both patients and dear friends.

Letterman Hospital, after being an outstanding medical facility at the Presidio for over one hundred years, closed in 1995. In its last few years, practically all of the medical treatment was for military retirees and their dependents. Many important people were treated at the medical hospital of Letterman during these last years. General of the army Omar Bradley and Mrs. Bradley were admitted for routine physicals. King Hussein of Jordan was also hospitalized there. Over the years Bob Hope and other dignitaries entertained the patients quite often.

INTERESTING HISTORY
OF VARIOUS WARS

Summary:

Only the Civil War, World War I and World War II had more service people die per year of each of the wars than in the Korean War! This includes all the other wars in our history.

ABOUT THE AUTHOR

Since leaving the army, and particularly S-1, my life has taken a much different direction. I wanted very much to become a medical doctor but I could not afford the cost. Soon my wife was expecting our first child and I had growing family responsibilities. So I became totally involved in the carpet and flooring industry. I went back to night school at the University of Minnesota and studied interior design. In fact, I ended up teaching some night classes at the university in interior design. Bev and I had four children. We moved numerous times as I was with the largest floor covering distributor in the world and was promoted over the next twenty years. Subsequently, I moved to Georgia and became head of a very large carpet manufacturer then started off a fledgling new carpet mill. Moving to Dallas, Texas, I owned a chain of retail floor covering stores. I sold these stores, moved back to Georgia, working with a new high-end national design center chain for a number of years. My wife, Bev, passed away after a long illness. Sometime later I met Stephanie and acquired a beautiful wife and two more children (grown). So we now have six children, fifteen grandchildren, and three great-grandchildren. I retired for a short time and painted a lot of happy paintings. Stephanie and I did some interior design consulting and then returned to the carpet business full time. We work and travel together throughout the USA and visit China, India, and other countries regularly in our business.

In closing, those nearly two years at S-1 stand out and definitely changed my life, particularly how I communicate and work with people over the years. I saw miracles occur in people with mental disease when they are treated with kindness, love, and true affection. The time at S-1 has directed and strengthened my personal Christian life and belief in the teachings of Jesus.

> And as ye would that men should do to you, do ye also to them likewise.
>
> Luke 6:31, KJV

Pat and Stephanie now reside in a suburb of Atlanta.